THE **COMING** **CYBER** WAR

THE **COMING**
CYBER WAR

WHAT EXECUTIVES, THE BOARD, AND YOU SHOULD KNOW

MARC CRUDGINGTON

The Coming Cyber War: What Executives, the Board, and You Should Know
by Marc Crudgington

1. COMPUTERS | Information Technology
2. COMPUTERS | Security | Network Security
3. BUSINESS & ECONOMICS | Information Management

ISBN (paperback)   978-1-7359163-0-9
ISBN (hardcover)   978-1-7359163-1-6
ISBN (ebook)   978-1-7359163-2-3

Library of Congress Control Number: 2020919953

Edited by: Tamma Ford
Cover and interior design by: Elena Reznikova, DTPerfect.com
Author photo by: Laura Giles, www.studio154photography.com

Published by CyberFore Systems, LLC
The Woodlands, Texas

Contact the author at: www.linkedin.com/in/marccrudgington

To my wife Maricris Crudgington
for continuing to allow me to indulge in 'side' endeavors,
for being supportive, and for being the best mom our boys
Jake and Luke could wish for.

To my sons Jake and Luke:
You two keep me striving to be a better father daily.
I could not ask for two sons that I love and enjoy any more
than you two. Keep dreaming bigger than you think possible…
and working hard to make those dreams a reality.

To all my family, thank you for being part of my life.

A portion of the proceeds from book sales will be donated to:
Disabled American Veterans (DAV) Charitable Service Trust and
The University of Texas MD Anderson Cancer Center

Contents

Confessions and Acknowledgements

THIS BOOK IS NOT FOR EVERYONE. NOR AM I PERFECT. This is my first book. For the most part, I did not get deep into the weeds about specific topics; some of those warrant a book in and of themselves. That was intentional: I wanted to write the book for a person who is not at all a cybersecurity practitioner as much as for the person who is. My intent was to make the book valuable reading for a C-level business executive, for an administrator and even for a student who may be thinking about a career in cybersecurity.

I believe even security practitioners will appreciate much of what is written. The goal of the book is to inform and raise the current cybersecurity awareness level so that we all may coalesce around a topic that crosses the political and functional divides.

Cybersecurity is of the utmost importance to our national security. My hope is that no matter who you are, that after reading *The Coming Cyber War*, you will feel called to action. At a minimum, I wish you to realize the importance of cybersecurity in your daily life, your business or place of work (including for stay-at-home moms who work as hard as anyone), and in much of the decision-making that you may do.

Like the cybersecurity field itself, no person can achieve great things on his own. Along my career path and in my life, I am reminded of the great Robert Frost Poem, *The Road Not Taken*. I have had many people who have helped me along the way.

To my two Yodas and close friends, Gerard Smith, and Alexis Rodriguez, after 30+ years of friendship (and many more to come) — THANK YOU!

Fellow CISOs in Houston Texas — you are a truly remarkable group of people and fighting the good fight. Your shared wisdom and the discussions we have had have added to me as a professional, whether that was a conversation in private, on a panel discussion together, or in a group setting. Our community is strong and only continues to get stronger. Let us up the collaboration and make Houston a model for all other CISO communities; let us be the catalyst to rename HOUSTON CYBER SPACE CITY.

CISOs and cybersecurity practitioners around the United States and globe — thank you for your shared knowledge and what you all do on a daily basis. So many great conversations have occurred while on a trip out of the Houston area. I especially would like to mention Colonel Cedric Leighton, a fellow Air Force veteran; thank you for sharing your knowledge and for the time you have spent with me.

To the CIOs and others from SIM Houston — what a great group of people to have discovered on my return to Houston! I recall like it was yesterday on my third day back in Houston, meeting two SIM members, Gene J. and Paul K., at a technology conference. We chatted, enjoyed our spirits of choice, and had many laughs. Those conversations continue to this day and with many more of you who are part of the Houston SIM Chapter. To each and every one of you — you and your wisdom are truly cherished.

All of the cybersecurity and technology partners and vendors that I have gotten to know in Houston and across the United States — thank you for your tireless efforts and friendships. Included in that group are all those who facilitate the wonderful conferences in Houston and around the US. I especially want to thank the team at T.E.N. for your dedication and heart; I will forever remember your kindness in Chicago during my foot surgery ordeal. It goes without saying that when you find a great cybersecurity partner, you will have a friend for life.

The InfraGard team in Houston, all of you, thank you for the countless hours you put in to make our chapter a success and the best InfraGard chapter on planet earth. From the presentations to the chapter meetings and the many events that draw in dedicated professionals, you are adding tremendous value to a cause that needs your perseverance. To our InfraGard Houston FBI Coordinators, AH, MM, BCG — wow, what a great leadership team we have been privileged with. You put your heart and soul into our community. THANK YOU!

The friends and colleagues I have gotten to know here in Houston Texas have been steady forces in my growth as a professional and a person. During Hurricane Harvey, our community came together like nobody has seen since 9/11. Two individuals provided direct help to me and my family during our time of need: Thank you, Marcus Lohr and Andy Paur; your kindness will never be forgotten. To other colleagues at Woodforest and the Texas Bankers Association and Texas banking community at large, thank you for your help during that time as well.

To Tamma Ford — I guess we should join in thanks to Al

Gore for creating the internet ... ha-ha, wink, wink! Thank you for your efforts in coaching me throughout the process of writing and editing this book.

To University of California, Irvine, Paul Merage School of Business EMBA 2008 fellow graduates, it's not quite running for President, but not too shabby. The Sea Rays still rock! ZOT ZOT ZOT!!!

For all others I may have missed, like that little ol' band from Texas, ZZ Top, said ... you didn't have to ... but you did, but you did, and I THANK YOU.

Introduction

Are We at (Cyber) War?

I T WAS JUNE 2016 AND THE DAY WAS ABSOLUTELY PICTUR-
esque. I had travelled into the Washington DC area for a
national cybersecurity conference that was being held in National
Harbor, Maryland. On that Sunday afternoon, the sun kissed
the Potomac River like a sailor returning from World War II
to meet his 'gal' on the docks of a United States Navy port.
As I took the ferry from National Harbor over to Old Town
Alexandria, Virginia, I marveled at our country's rich history
with its glorious monuments and wonderous landscape. Gazing
across the horizon of the Potomac — the United States Capitol
Building, the Washington Monument, the Lincoln Memorial,
the Thomas Jefferson Memorial, Arlington National Cemetery,
and The George Washington Masonic National Memorial, with
glimpses of the White House — all right there to remind me
of our freedoms and values. It was going to be a wonderful trip
and I was very excited for the week to come when I would see

old acquaintances, be introduced to new ones, participate in the many sessions on cybersecurity, and meet with vendors that I am partnered with.

I was especially excited to catch up that evening in Old Town Alexandria with my friend Colonel Cedric Leighton whom I had met a few years earlier at another conference. Col. Leighton is a United States Air Force veteran like myself and is very knowledgeable about military intelligence, geopolitical events, and cybersecurity due to his 26-year career in the Air Force as an intelligence officer and serving as a Deputy Director of the National Security Agency during his last military assignment. Before meeting Col. Leighton, I was going to soak in the beauty of the day on the docks of Old Town Alexandria Harbor and decompress from a hectic flight and hotel check-in.

Having been involved in cybersecurity, intelligence, and computer communications while serving, I contemplated the news of that spring and early summer with the 2016 election in full swing. There were grumblings of Russian interference in our election through a variety of cyber techniques and campaigns such as social media, stolen emails, and manufactured ads. These are the kind of stories Washington DC eats up and this election cycle was shaping up to be one to remember. As I thought back on the history of information security and cybersecurity, I wondered how far we had come from being able to protect the nation's critical assets with just a "firewall".

Cyber defenses and Chief Information Security Officers (CISOs — pronounced 'SEE-SO') were now playing a critical role in an entity's survival and in creating/preserving shareholder value. Some CISOs were even garnering Board seats or a presenter's seat at the Board table. Now we were building out intricate cyber defenses with multiple layers woven together. These defenses included threat intelligence, network defenses, access controls, endpoint security, logging systems, user awareness training, deceptive techniques, frameworks, plans, policies, processes, regulations and many other tools in defense of an entity's infrastructure, all designed to keep the 'bad guys' out. (And rest assured, that is the sole mention of these "geeky" tools I will make in these pages).

Yet in spite of our defensive tools, the breaches were still mounting. The bad guys were getting in, whether at Target, Saudi Aramco, LinkedIn, Yahoo, or the United States Office of Personnel Management… among tens of thousands of others. Were we going about it all wrong? Was it one little weakness we were missing that allowed the threat actor to gain a foothold? And since we all know that technology is evolving at the speed of light, what would the future of cybersecurity and cyberattacks look like?

As I sat relaxing, my mind raced on the incredible opportunity there was ahead and the overwhelming nature of this daunting crisis. At that time, I believed that we were just at the beginning of what cyber had to offer. We were in the 1st inning of a ballgame and yes, there were major league players involved from every major company and every nation in the world. There were billions of dollars' worth of intellectual property, data, and countless reputations at stake.

My discussions that evening at Fish Market Restaurant with Col. Leighton were rich in topic. Yes, we caught up on our personal lives with our usual, "How is your family? How is work? You doing okay? How are the speaking engagements going? I saw you on CNN the other day — great talk." Our attention turned to the election news cycle, cybersecurity, geopolitical events, Executive Orders pertaining to cybersecurity, and other matters of the cyber world. Both of us had spent years in computers and cybersecurity in one aspect or another. Our conversation kept coming back to the velocity and scope of breaches, the nature and origin of the threat actors behind them, and the escalating geopolitical influences on cyberattacks. The rising cyber risks were everywhere and all entities — whether of the government or private sector, small business, or large corporation, wealthy or poor, young, or old — were susceptible to some type of cyberattack or data privacy event.

Cedric and I could have talked into the wee hours of the morning. The computer age had gone from a few connected researchers and government networks to an explosion of interconnected devices, applications, systems, companies, and countries. The world was connected and so tightly coupled that one could launch a devastating attack against any New York based Fortune 500 company and cripple its network and websites in the matter of minutes — and do it from a dilapidated building in a third world country halfway around the globe.

Our digital capabilities and usage have exploded in a short time. Email took off, from the first single message sent and received in the 1960s to over 293.6 billion sent and received daily among over 4 billion users in 2019. The Internet has over 4.54 billion active users creating 88,555GB of traffic every second of the day via more than 362.3 million registered domain names and 1.75 billion websites. Commerce on the internet has grown exponentially and is predicted to generate $6.54T in sales per year by 2021. In 2019, there were over 26 billion active IoT (Internet of Things) devices installed worldwide and by 2025, it is predicted there will be more the 75 billion such devices in use. From home speakers, TVs, refrigerators and other home appliances to cars and other vehicle types to the most critical infrastructure devices running our nuclear power plants, we are now a tightly connected world.

I come back to my special topic and area of expertise. For all the aspirations, wonder, and amazing potential the internet and technology bring to the world, it is also bringing chaos, anxiety, destruction, crime, and fear when used with malicious intent. It has also brought a new type of arms race, the cyber arms race. Mark Clayton wrote for The Christian Science Monitor, "*Tomorrow's wars will be fought not just with guns, but with the click of a mouse half a world away that will unleash weaponized software that could take out everything from the power grid to a chemical plant.*" It may surprise you to know that that article was published in March 2011; think of how far we have come in tighter interconnectedness, technological developments, and vaster cyber warfare capabilities since that date.

The capabilities, anxieties, and concerns have merged to create an industry that is worth approximately $173 billion in 2020 and predicted to grow to $270 billion by 2026. The industry is called *Cyber Security*. Corporations spent $5.6B on cloud security in 2018 and are predicted to more than double that in 5 years for a spend of $12.6B in 2023. Government agencies have now been created to defend against cyberattacks at all levels of government — national, state, municipal. The Cybersecurity & Infrastructure Security Agency was created in 2018 as a new federal agency to protect the nation's critical infrastructure through the Cybersecurity and Infrastructure Security Agency Act of 2018. Cybersecurity and the job of protecting the United States' assets crosses all political lines and is deemed as one of America's greatest needs. Numerous military cyber groups have been created to help defend our national interest throughout the globe with the United States Cyber Command (created in 2009, it is the primary military entity). Cyber warfare is taking place like an ocean current; you don't really see it but feel it if you are caught in it. In some respects, it is also obvious.

On my short journey back to National Harbor, I looked back
on my journey in technology and cybersecurity wondering how
a small-town (Onalaska, Texas) kid would end up in Washington
DC talking to one of the United States' most knowledgeable
figures on global geopolitical, strategic, leadership, management,
and cybersecurity topics. Memories of me deciding to study computers in college, learning computer engineering on an 8088
processor, my decision to join the United States Air Force, time
spent in Silicon Valley, getting my MBA in southern California
at the University of California Irvine, and then moving back to
Houston Texas were as vivid as the day I made each decision.
The progression all made sense: *"Two roads diverged in a wood,
and I — I took the one less traveled by, and that has made all the
difference"* — Robert Frost, The Road Not Taken.

I also thought — with all of these cyber capabilities and continuing escalations across the globe — that no greater threat exists
on earth to destroy an individual, an enterprise, a country, our
world than the power of cyber warfare.

Cyber Warriors, Cyber Novices, and "Isn't this just a bunch of Star Wars stuff?"

Try to talk to someone at a party about cyberspace and cybersecurity and you are likely to either make an instant friend or to
receive a 'deer in the headlights' glazed look. People's knowledge
about cyberspace and cybersecurity ranges from those with a
vast comprehension of the topic to those that are aware of how
to protect themselves at home and keep a careful watch on their
data... to those still have trouble setting the clock on their mi-
crowave. It is true!

Technology is everywhere and proliferates throughout society at a pace that can sometimes be mindboggling. Let us look at learning for an illustration of this pace. People nearing or in retirement today probably never used a computer in school, even when in college. While completing my MBA in 2006-2008, we were introduced to the option of attending classes via the internet if we could not make it in person for any reason. Twelve years later, in 2020, with the Coronavirus pandemic in full swing, kids of all ages were able to move fairly seamlessly into remote learning via Zoom or other online meeting technologies. Seamless, because most of those kids have grown up with a smartphone and internet connectivity in their hands. Both formal and informal learning can be acquired online whether it is through a paying elite university platform or through a free social media or website platform.

My point is that just about anything can be done utilizing the internet and cyberspace — and it is. This opens us all up to wonderous opportunities but also puts us at risks from having our private data stolen and posted for viewing or for sale on the dark web (and this can include our medical, financial, or personally identifying information). Despite the fact that many of us perform medical transactions, financial transactions, and freely provide our data to complete strangers over the internet via personal devices, we still do not understand cybersecurity. We still do not utilize basic cybersecurity hygiene practices when performing these tasks.

In the first six months of 2019, more than 4 billion records were exposed in data breaches. In December 2019, a single researcher discovered over one billion plain text passwords exposed on an unsecure database — for anyone to view and acquire. A look at the list of the 100 worst passwords actually used in 2019

(12345, 123456, 123456789, test1, password) will demonstrate the need for us to become more cyber-aware.

Have no doubt: These types of practices carry over from our home computer and personal smartphone usage to the enterprise and government usage. Need proof? Just look at phishing statistics for the average company where many an employee falls victim to a phishing simulation exercise being done by cyber criminals.

> *"Cybersecurity is a shared responsibility, and it boils down to this: in cybersecurity, the more systems we secure, the more secure we all are. We are all connected online and a vulnerability in one place can cause a problem in many other places. So, everyone needs to work on this: government officials and business leaders, security professionals and utility owners and operators."*

These are the remarks of Department of Homeland Security Secretary Jeh Johnson speaking about the release of the Cybersecurity Framework in February 2014. The Cybersecurity Framework is not just for government. What Secretary Johnson was trying to convey in his remarks is what is on the minds of many in the United States and globally. Catastrophic events, disruptions to critical infrastructure, and battles between militaries will no longer just be carried out by missiles, bombs, and guns, but with cyber weapons that can quickly cripple the most physically fortified structures built. The much-mediatized Stuxnet and its deployment to wreak havoc on an Iranian uranium enrichment plant was a sample of what is to come.

Our country and all its citizens must start to take cyber threats and cybersecurity seriously or we risk dire consequences. To be blatantly repetitive, technology is everywhere and accessible by anyone with a mobile phone and a few bars of connectivity. Cybersecurity protects our identities, allows us to conduct private financial transactions, helps us protect intellectual property of all types ranging from the location of the next undiscovered oil reservoir to the blueprints of your Internet-connected heart monitor or pacemaker.

All of us use this type of data and devices on a daily basis. To combat the growing threats, we must expand the offering of cyber classes in our high schools and junior highs; Technology should be a required subject for graduation like English, History, Math or Foreign Language requirements.

We should each become self-aware of basic cyber hygiene and practice it daily. Our obligation is not to pass the buck of security to the next generation or to the company's younger staff, but to lean in and understand it as a matter of National Security. We should encourage our children to explore a career in technology and cybersecurity. Here they have vast opportunities to become our Cyber Warriors of the future and defend against The Coming Cyber War.

How I came to write "The Coming Cyber War"

Certainly, for some that know me, this may seem like something that I would rather talk about amongst a group of friends, acquaintances, or at a conference than write about. I was voted most likely to run for President by my UCI Paul Merage School of Business EMBA 2008 classmates and we all know politicians like to talk.

However, those that really know me are not surprised at all that I decided to write a book. If you had told me while I was in high school that one day, I'd be writing a professional business book, I would have said you are crazy. But, if you would have told that to one of my good friends, he would have probably said, "I can see that happening." Oh, the things we wish we knew then that we know now.

The idea really started crystalizing a little over four years ago in 2016. At that time, I was fascinated by the growth in cybersecurity and the opportunities in the field that were starting to be visible on the horizon. Additionally, I was becoming keenly aware of the nature of cyber escalations and nation state cyberattacks. As time went on, I began to realize how even some of the greatest business minds in our society failed to grasp some of the basic concepts of cybersecurity. Nor did they seem to know what they should about developing, participating in, or providing oversight to a strong cybersecurity program.

As I traveled around the country attending cybersecurity conferences, I found myself listening to great leaders like General Colin Powell, Secretary Leon Panetta, General Keith Alexander, and many others who were discussing their growing concern about cybersecurity, cyber warfare. They were sharing the actions our country (including citizens) should be taking to address cyber risk. Yet, breach after breach, some of the most basic concepts were overlooked or failed . . . causing a headline-making catastrophe.

Over the course of the four-plus year journey from, "I should write a book" to writing a LinkedIn article, which nearly became only a Tweet, to finally writing this book, I had countless interactions with my peers from across the US and globe. They ranged from Fortune 500 companies to community banks of Texas. From large global security firms to startup company founders asking for my insight on their product. From conference founders to conference Program Managers. From fellow attendees of the FBI CISO Academy to fellow attendees of intimate dinners around

Houston, Texas. From CEOs and other CISOs to analyst level security practitioners that are in the fight day in and day out. And of course, my Houston, Texas peers and acquaintances that make our cybersecurity community so special. Throughout that journey, I engaged and listened intently to their thoughts, their concerns about the industry, and read and discussed with them the latest breach or topic of cyber news choice.

Throughout these conversations, there seemed to be a few central themes that would come back again and again:

- **Cyberattacks:** Everyone was becoming more aware of the growing velocity, scope, and sophistication of some of the breaches that were occurring. If the Target Corporation breach woke people up, the Sony breach and Equifax breach shocked them. It almost seemed as if we were becoming numb to the escalating numbers and scope of breaches. The shift in how entities designed their cybersecurity programs echoed the sentiments of peers: Detection and Response were just as important as Protection.

- **Talent:** Closing the talent gap is a real conundrum for businesses, industry, government, and the military. The number of open cyber jobs (that is, unfilled because the right qualified candidates are just not applying) is clearly outstripping the numbers of qualified people out there on the job market. There is a lot of opportunity in the cyber industry now and not just for engineers and analysts, but for specialists taking cyber-care of Marketing, Sales, Finance, Program and Project Management, HR, and other internet-facing disciplines.

- **Cyber Resources:** The talent shortage is not only due to lack of people but of top-grade resources in our cyber defense efforts. It is due to a lack in truly beneficial security systems and other resources that save us and our colleagues' time, prevent alert fatigue (*alert fatigue* is a state of becoming desensitized to safety *alerts*), and help us mitigate the breach-to-breach-response-gap (or *dwell time*).

- **Organization Undercurrents:** The dynamics between a CISO, the other C-suite executives and members of the Board can be perplexing to many. Many CISOs are techies at heart and business acumen does not come easy to them. This is due to no fault of their own; it is just not a strength. The converse is that many Boards and other Executives understand the business, but do not speak tech. This creates an opportunity for both sides to become "bilingual" and to bridge that language barrier. Also, whether it is what CISOs put in their board reports, how they 'sell' security to the board and C-suite, or the interactions they may be having with their fellow executives, cyber security discussions come up frequently and both parties need to learn enough to effectively communicate with reasonable comfort on these business-security matters.

It is with my observations and desire to do something crazy (write a book) that I set out on this journey. Well not really. See, it is August 2020, and we are in the middle of a pandemic so … it is a choice to either watch my grass grow or to write a book. Ha-ha! Kidding, but somewhat true. I really wanted to tackle these themes as well as questions such as:

- Where do we go from here? Indeed, where are cyber threat actors taking us?

- What should executives and the Board understand about cyber space and cyber security matters? Cyber threat actors won't go away; we need to be proactive in our defenses.

- What do people need to know about their internet-facing world to help reduce risks? Attention to safety is a matter for all of us who are internet connected in any way.

- What are some of the motivating factors involved? Threat actors know why they are tapping at your door. Why are you taking defensive measures against their breaches? What do you need to protect?

- Why does it really matter? The answers will come from discussions with your colleagues and peers, your customers and partners, your in-house personnel and your virtual workforce...

With my four-plus years to dwell on these thoughts, mountains of notes, and a bit of extra time on my hands due to the pandemic, I was all in and ready to go.

Cyber security is not for the weak at heart. It can be hell, raise hell in the ranks and in the boardroom, and be painful as hell.

Here is the truth, though: *It affects all of us in every aspect of our lives now. All of us need to care. We all need to tackle this problem. We all start by acquiring knowledge.*

Cyber risks and cyber issues are around us all every day of our lives and everywhere we turn. It affects how we make political, businesses, and personal decisions. There are certainly contrasting cyber-matters to consider and the decisions to be made about them cause us to wring our hands:

- Individual privacy of data versus protecting data

- from federal laws to state laws to personal responsibility

- the trade-off between accepting risks or increasing costs to reduce them

- to build a cyber army at the expense of a physical one or not

We face these dilemmas, and more are growing day by day. Now is the time as a nation that we must act, and act together.

This book is decidedly not meant to be an 'in the weeds' dissection of malware or the most detailed intricacies of tactics, techniques, and procedures used by cyber bad guys and the cyber good guys, though it contains some of that. It is intended to enlighten all executives, members of all Boards, and you about what is needed. My goal is to raise the level of understanding on why it matters.

It is my hope that you find this book fulfilling and educational. Just maybe it will pique your interest enough to encourage your child, grandchild, or other family to seek out a career in cyber security. May it raise your level of awareness about the industry and The Coming Cyber War.

PART ONE

Cyber Space
& The Cyber War

I T IS AMAZING TO ME, EVEN THOUGH I AM IN THE WEEDS of such things every day, that people cannot define in so many words what cyberspace is all about. It will be my job in the next few chapters to clarify that for you.

Cyber breaches, massive thefts of digitally stored data, ransoms of millions of dollars over digital databases and operational access are all more frequently the subject of media coverage than ever. However, I also find that people in leadership roles don't know the scope of risks of their internet-facing information.

If the organization's leaders do not understand the scope of risk to their data and information, their Intellectual Property, their customer databases, their internet-facing transactional security are faced with, they cannot move to mediate or eliminate those risks. This is my call to business owners, C-Suite executives, Board directors, government, and community leadership to expand your education on cyber risks, cyber defenses and cybersecurity programs.

The cyber war is upon us and we need to suit up, arm ourselves with knowledge, the most effective cyber-defensive and cyber-offensive weaponry we can devise, and prepare to face cyber criminals head on. It is not a scenario for a sci-fi movie. It is not a conspiracy theory to debunk. It is not an action-thriller novel. It is what you are surrounded with right now in your business, in your schools, in your community and in your homes. Let's gear up and defend ourselves.

Chapter 1

What Is Cyber Space?

NOT EVERYONE IS FULLY AWARE OF EVERYTHING THAT comprises "cyber space" or even how long it has been part of the way we do business, govern the nation, and live our personal lives.

Cyberspace is the single word we use to describe our global, interconnected digital technologies. Cyberspace is where communication takes place between and amongst people over computer networks.

Cyberspace is a global, interdependent network of information infrastructures which include the Internet, the World Wide Web, the deep web, the dark web, our telecommunications networks, all our networked computer systems, and the embedded processors and controllers that give us the information we want with a keyboard click.

Cyberspace is also people, of course, creating and navigating in an environment with no physical form — a virtual space. It is a symbolic place. It is not a literal place or space at all, but figurative.

Cyberspace is made tangible to us through our various technology devices (hardware such as computers, smartphones, servers, etc.) and their software and services.

Cyberspace is thus the flow of digitized information between and among networked computers. When we talk of being online, we are referring to cyberspace more than the internet; we refer to the virtual or intangible sharing of information via our devices. It is where one moment we can be on a mountaintop viewing not the vast natural vista before our eyes but a TikTok video (even making and sharing one for that matter); listening to our favorite music channel via Spotify on the way down that mountain; entertaining the kids with their favorite animated feature film on a drive home from that country excursion.

The Internet

The internet. The information superhighway. The worldwide web, or web. A global information system. Pervasive networking.

The internet has evolved tremendously — both technologically and socially — since the 1960s. By 1985, the internet was fairly firmly established as a technology used by researchers (academic and governmental) and technology developers. The rule of free and open access meant that developers from anywhere in the world could (and did) contribute to its expansion, and it became both a collection of technologies and a collection of communities as it moved out of a pure research world and into the mainstream in the 1990s.

There is a difference between cyberspace and the internet. The internet exists within cyberspace. The internet is a network of networks, the interconnection of networks — inter*(connection* *of)* net*(works)*. Your corporation's private network co-resides on the internet along with all other corporations' networks, and alongside government and military networks. It is your mechanism for sharing, storing, and collecting information in your business; it is connection and communication with the world outside your company.

The internet has a global broadcasting capability, but there is no global control at the operations level. Note that there is a school of thinkers believing that anything, once 'posted' on the internet, is public domain material when its owners do not agree. That is one reason that cyber ethics and cyber law is under discussion around the world today — where unfettered free speech, copyright protection of one's work including ownership of software, definitions and protections for intellectual property, nation state censorship privilege and other matters are hot topics for actors as high as government ministers and heads of state.

It is over the internet that we send emails and share photos, play virtual games, build, and operate an eCommerce business, and where we socialize (thus the term *social* media) remotely with each other. The world wide web (the WWW in our website names) is built upon the internet but is not the internet.

Who Is in Control of the Web?

It is October 1, 2016. The US government handed over control of the world wide web's 'phonebook' to the Internet Corporation for Assigned Names and Numbers (ICANN) on this date. This transition was in the works for 20 years. Prior to that, could we say the US 'owned' the web? No. The 'phonebook' for the web is the DNS or domain name system. ICANN is the organization that now assigns numerical internet addresses to websites and computers and then translates them into the alphabet-based web addresses that people type into their browsers. The phonebook is henceforth managed by this nonprofit organization.

Here is some cocktail party novelty for you, and you can probably be sure that 1) people will believe you are making this up and 2) that you will be called a conspiracy buff even if they want to believe you:

If a party were to gain control of ICANN's database or phonebook, that party could control the internet. That party could send users to fake bank or financial websites instead of the real ones and take over the real one with no one the wiser (for a while, at least, and that little moment is all a hacker needs). Multiply that by the types and numbers of disruptions and you see that this is how anyone "owns" the world wide web.

Rest easy, though: the ICANN database can be rebuilt. ICANN devised a multi-actor method to protect the internet and its phonebook. This serves to put the internet squarely in a multiple-stakeholder model of governance — it is under a more decentralized control than first appears to be the case. ICANN selected seven real individuals from around the world as key holders. This refers to real physical keys — the 'keys to the web kingdom' as it were. ICANN assigned an additional seven individuals to serve as backups, for a total of 14 people who "control or own the world wide web".

Why a physical key? Each one goes to a real bank-held safe deposit box, and the various boxes are located around the world. Inside those safe deposit boxes are 'smart' key cards. Put the seven of them together and you have the 'master' key, which is not in this case yet another physical key, but computer code or a password to the phonebook.

Note the reactions you get with your story at the cocktail party. This is the stuff of political action movies and spy novels...

Web or Net?

The Internet (or just the 'net') links your computer to other computers around the world. It transports your data, your images or other digital content.

It is the world wide web (web) that lets you use that content. The web runs your visible content on the underlying invisible Internet.

You don't need the internet to run your business's intranet, since by definition it runs on your in-house server. It is a closed, private network — but don't relax your vigilance. It can be hacked and be riddled with malicious software, viruses, or worms. You need to apply everything you learn in these pages to your intranet (your VPN) and to your more public, internet-driven systems.

Are there other parts to the internet besides the world wide web? Yes, the web has an invisible brother, called the Deep Web. It also has a shadowy sister, called the Dark Web. Before diving into the 'dark web', first learn about the 'deep web'.

The Deep Web

The World Wide Web just discussed is also called the 'surface web' in contrast to the 'deep web'.

Also called the invisible web or the hidden web, the deep web is a huge part of the internet you can readily access, but search engines won't bring you to the pages here. The deep web refers to the massive number of pages and places not indexed by the web's commercial search engines such as Google or Mozilla Firefox.

We have, however, all quite legally and ethically been here — and sometimes spend most of our computer time here whether we are at work or at play.

You are in the deep web when you sign into your bank account online with your username and password. Once on that password protected page, you are in an unindexed location — on the deep web. You are also on the deep web when you communicate with other people through private social media pages, chat services and messaging platforms. If you are using a paid service such as video on demand or online magazines, the deep web is where you land after you log in; you go behind the paywall, to an unindexed page, to access content.

Deep web pages are assigned URLs or IP addresses — you can type in the deep web URL, but no content will be available until you log in as a bona fide user.

The deep web is bigger and has much larger activity than the surface web. Mainstream search engines and other developers have begun exploring alternative methods to index the deep web, but it is still for the future.

The Dark Web

In your reading about cyberspace, you probably never heard of the 'deep web', but the 'dark web' has long been a thing of conspiratorial whispers. Hear someone refer to the dark web and it conjures up images of covert criminality, meeting places for international hackers, deep secrecy, and anonymity. All that is part of the dark web, but not the whole of it.

'Dark net, backweb, onionweb' all refer to the dark web.

NOTE: Don't be too nonchalant about the dark web or skip this information because "you'll never use the dark web".

When your corporation's data or your family or personal data has been stolen, it ends up for sale there, on the dark web. If your system has been hacked or infected, the sources of that disruption are on the dark web. When your company is hostage to a ransomware demand, the hacker are communicating with each other about your business's vulnerabilities via the dark web. They are comparing notes and setting the ransom amount based on insider information another hacker lifted from your data.

Understanding the dark web is a key to protecting your company, your employees and clients, those partners in your supply chain, yourself, and family from risks. Understanding the dark web is vital to being cyber secure anywhere in the digital space you navigate.

The dark web functions, as does the World Wide Web, with a search engine and websites. Dark web sites look other sites you typically use on the web once you are on their pages, but with some notable differences.

The first thing that sets them visibly apart is their naming structure. Instead of ending in .com, .co, .net or .org, dark web sites end in .onion. This domain suffix designates an 'anonymous hidden service'. The .onion sites can be accessed via an anonymizing browser such as the Tor search engine (searching only the dark web for you) which requires registration and login by users. And that is a second distinction of the dark web — you are there anonymously. Unlike commercial or mainstream browsers that can track you, once logged in to the dark web via Tor, you are invisible.

In short, you cannot reach a dark website through ordinary browsers such as Google or Mozilla, and using Tor keeps you anonymous. (There have been attempts to create competing dark web browsers to Tor, but users have found them unreliable. Tor is the go-to browser and the standard its competitors try to but have not been able to match.)

Another difference between the surface web and the dark web is in website URLs. Dark web sites use a scrambled naming structure creating URLs that are typically impossible to remember. For example, a popular dark web commerce site called *Dream Market* goes by the unintelligible address of 'eajwlvm3z2lcca76.onion.'

Finally, you have to know where to go to get to a dark web page or site and might consult a master file provided by an organization known as the Hidden Wiki. The file will not tell you if a site performs illegal services, however; that knowledge will be up to you to discover.

It is not illegal per se to access the dark web: The dark web in and of itself is not illegal. Both legal and illegal activities, services and transactions take place there. Many go there due to its anonymity. But make no mistake: The dark web is all about web-surfer-beware.

As examples of legal activities, political and sports forums and blogs exist on the dark web. Using them is perfectly legal; that is, they are legal unless they are hosted and cater to citizens of nation states practicing censorship of such things. Dark sites might cater to people whose ideologies are not for just any eyes or ears. Facebook has a legal site on the dark web. Law enforcement organizations and journalists are legitimate users of the onionweb.

As to illegality, weapons and arms, drugs and hacking services are available for sale on the dark web, and would definitely be viewed as illegal were, they to try to publish a World Wide Web site for the same purposes. If it is an illegal product, service, transaction, or topic (such as hate topics or incitement to criminality), you find it on the dark web. eBay-like sites (the Silk Road is an example that the FBI took down in 2013) facilitate peer-to-peer criminality and criminal transactions such as buying/selling illegal physical goods and illegal services. That includes the buying/selling of your stolen data.

Dark web users' number in the millions. Dark web users call the World Wide Web the 'clearnet' in obvious contrast to what cannot be seen on the dark web.

The Cloud

Another aspect of cyberspace is the Cloud. There is a lot of ink implying that we have shifted recently to the cloud and leading many to think that the cloud and cloud computing is a newer phenomenon than it is. While its use has mushroomed, it in fact dates back four decades: If you remember AOL as a web portal and online service provider, that was one of the early cloud applications.

What is the 'Cloud'? While the word 'cloud' is rather vague, it just means 'housed on someone else's computer or server instead of your own'. It also means 'accessible from anywhere you have an internet connection'. Cloud computing is on-demand availability of computer system resources, especially today as regards storing and accessing your data from any internet-connected device or accessing more computing power.

Differently stated, the cloud represents 1) servers located in 'data centers' all over the world, managed by third parties, and that are accessed over the Internet 2) the software and databases that run from/are stored on those servers.

The advantage of cloud computing is clearly that users and companies don't have to manage and maintain physical servers themselves in their homes or places of business. They don't even have to run software applications on their own computers. As an example of the latter, Microsoft 365 is cloud-hosted packages of the company's widely-used office software applications; the initial downside in legacy MS Office users' minds was 'no internet connection, no access to the MS software', as the programs no longer reside on each local computer hard drive.

Clouds are public or private. Clouds are private to your corporation if you have the capacity or the budget for it, and you might outsource its management and maintenance or do so internally. Public or shared cloud service is where many smaller-need users unknown to each other are using a managed space; public clouds might be free.

Public cloud service providers include Amazon Web Services, IBM Cloud, Oracle, Microsoft, Google, and Alibaba. They own and operate their data center infrastructure.

Cloud service models are beginning to grow with additional models such as Storage as a Service (STaaS), Security as a Service (SECaaS), and Data as a Service (DaaS) among others. The three primary models are Software as a Service (SaaS), Platform as a Service (PaaS), and Infrastructure as a Service (IaaS).

Software as a Service is an application delivered over the Internet by the application provided; it is also known as hosted services. Examples would include Gmail, Salesforce and Slack, among others.

Platform as a Service is a computing platform — the operating system and other services — delivered as a service over the Internet by the service provider. Examples would be Amazon Web Services Elastic Beanstalk, Magento Commerce Cloud, Windows Azure, and other services.

Infrastructure as a Service is a virtualized computing environment delivered as a service over the Internet by the service provider. Examples of this model would be Amazon Web Services, Microsoft Azure, Rackspace, among others.

Among the earliest commercial uses for the cloud was providing a place for a company to host its applications and services for the public. Next came cloud data storage. Your business paid a flat monthly fee or a pay-for-volume fee to house your data on someone else servers — your data was stored on a server or set of servers 'off-site' from your own place of business. Today's cloud-based data centers give businesses with data in the cloud a real scalability in both upward and downward directions; when your business and the related amount of data grows, so does your 'space' in the cloud and when it shrinks you can likewise adjust cloud services.

There is a collaborative reason that the cloud is popular. You can allow access by multiple simultaneous users to the same data set. With efficiencies and redundancy inherent, you can grant levels of access to employees and offices you have around the world, and make sure that everyone is following the same business mission and using vetted go-to-market tactics and so on — from one monitor.

Chapter 2

Cybercrime Is Global

"We have one or more <u>adversaries</u> breaching us."

THAT SHOULD BE YOUR FIRST THOUGHT WHEN THE TEAM (or a client) says, "There's a problem in the system". Your role is to realize that one or more of your business's adversaries has found a way into your house. Ask yourself, though, if they are not already *in* the house! For though it is a global activity, we will see in the next pages that insider threat actors are far from rare and not always innocent. Thus, your adversaries may be domestic or international business competitors, insiders, nation states, individual cyber criminals.

Cybercrime is about intention; your organization has been intentionally breached for a (perhaps not yet known) nefarious reason. Cybercrime groups are organized and respect no national boundaries. They certainly, by definition, do not respect the notion of privacy.

Same Criminals, New Tactics

Some age-old or more traditional types of crime, while still with us, have also gone digital, and must be counted as new types of risk you face:

- The Nigerian scams used to arrive in your snail-mailbox as a simple one-page letter; now they are digitized and arrive in your email box or hit you over social media chats.

- Ransoms typically bring kidnapping to mind, where a real person is seized and held for a high amount of cash to buy his release; now criminals seize and hold your business's digital data in exchange for a huge cash sum.

- The big-city pickpocket will always roam the streets and drop a light hand into your bag or pocket; now, though, a casual passerby may have digitally and remotely copied the credit cards in your wallet, while smiling at you as he passes.

- The sale of counterfeit trademarked products (or 'knock-offs') has always been a commercial risk. We find a 'cheap' Rolex or Gucci bag on the market and scoop it up. Such knockoffs now extend from medical products and electronics to automobile parts and fashion items; the theft and counterfeiting is rampant, wide-ranging and costs trademark and brand owners billions every year in lost sales and legal fees for remedial actions.

Today such counterfeiting has expanded, as your digital forms of your blueprints, research, formulas, designs, and other Intellectual Property are stolen from your computer system or from those of your own licensed manufacturers. Intellectual property is not seen as private property or a corporate asset, but as an easily accessible open-market commodity for sale and resale by cyberthieves. (Think of pirated software, pirated digitized DVD movies, stolen formulas, or engineering blueprints, etc.).

Common Cybercrimes

Cybercrimes, by definition, are digital in nature, computer-committed and internet powered. They are initiated from anywhere on globe and remote from you — or occur from just down the hall from your own office. All types of cybercrime are highly hazardous to your business's health.

Organized cybercrime is wide ranging, and it is impossible in an overview book such as this to list all the types of cybercrimes, vandalism, and disruptions your organization (or indeed your own household) may experience. Thus, your focus should not only be on criminal activities affecting your business, but also those potentially affecting your personal digital life and that of your family and especially the children in your charge.

For now, let's break down the major types of cybercrime that your business organization might have to prevent or remedy. We'll see about your personal digital risks later in these pages.

Hackers. These are individuals with sophisticated, high level computer programming skills as a rule. As stated elsewhere, hacking is a crime that has various roots, done out of curiosity to test one's high level programming skills, to show off, or done from greed or desire for power over a person or company.

The outcome is that your software and data are modified/distorted, stolen/locked up, misused. These malicious hackers will steal your unwary system administrator's or other master passcodes to access your system with apparent authorization. Your system might be modified to allow a hacker later access when he will insert his own code, track/steal your data, or execute other tasks he has programmed for later occurrence. Hackers intent on destruction are called either 'crackers' or 'black hat' hackers (aka the bad guys).

Skilled hackers who act out of curiosity and whose ethics are against the criminal abuse and misuse of others' systems might be the ones you hire to analyze, test your systems for flaws and weaknesses. These professionals you hire to break in/attempt to break into your system in view to "patching up the holes" are called 'white hat' hackers (aka the good guys).

Viruses, worms, malware. Cybercrime can start as cyber vandalism — destruction or other tampering with your servers or computers — introducing viruses, worms/malware, or Trojan programs, as well as squatting or taking over a computer remotely and secretly. A virus attaches itself to your files or documents and tends to migrate or infect other files and computers. A worm does not attach but self-replicates to gobble up the memory in your system.

Worms and viruses are related malware or malicious software, while Trojan horses are a bit different. They pretend to be legitimate files that you might attach to an email or download from a website. These have been created intentionally to gain access to your digital property and steal it from you, or to disrupt your system's ability to function.

Logic bombs are a type of malware which is programmed to trigger at a specific event or condition; the version of this that executes at a specific day/time is called a time bomb that then explodes and begins to replicate itself in your system. Email bombs and spamming operate similarly to flood your email account and crash it.

Fraud. Credit card fraud and identity theft is well known and often discussed in mainstream media. For cyber criminals of any level of skill, it is open season every hour of the day on identity documents of all kinds: Financial and health information, social security numbers, passports, driver licenses, voter registration cards, as well as data stored on your company and personal smartphones are all at risk all the time. Malware is used to collect computer users' passwords, and from there to gain access into databases of all types, stealing your personal banking information and other saleable data.

Denial-of-service (DoS). This encompasses distributed denial of service (DDoS) as well. The express intention is to deny service or block access to authorized or intended users of that service. It involves overwhelming a computer website or other resource with a floodtide of requests than it cannot handle, resulting in server overload. When someone says "The server crashed" you might in fact have suffered a DoS.

Web jacking. Hackers take over your website and make changes to it to sabotage your business or to profit themselves.

Phishing. This crime steals passwords or credit card information by posing as the legitimate company with which you do business. You might receive an email (voicemail or websites) appearing authentic and respond to it, giving up account or password information that allows cybercriminals to use it themselves or sell it forward. A clue that it is phishing is misspelled words or poor grammar in the message. Another hint might come if you first hover over a URL the hacker wants you click to see if it is actually the same one printed.

Dark web ecommerce. Ecommerce is a big playground for cybercriminals. They sell illicitly gained products and illegal services from ecommerce webstore formats — ones that look legitimate on the world wide web and ones that are less clearly legal on the dark web.

Trafficking and terrorism. Cybercrime reaches beyond what we think of as corporate and personal information theft and disruption, to include drug and human trafficking, international and regional terrorism. Cybercrimes against people include online stalking or spying (online predators work against both adults and minor children), and creation and distribution of child pornography.

At What Cost?

In 2018, global cyber criminals clicked a few keys — and stole $1.5T away from legitimate businesses, unassuming individuals, and government entities. For 2021, $6T in cybercrime damages will be the worldwide burden.

Don't wave off that big number thinking your "little business" or your "particular industry" is not at risk, and so why get all excited? At an average cost in the US of $8.19M per breach — or a cost per lost record of $150 — some businesses already know they would fold under the liability (and too many smaller businesses really do, and within six months of such breaches). How many records does your business possess? Do the math and shudder... The costs of data breaches are impossible to cover in one payment or one annual budget. They may persist on your business's ledgers for years and even decades before you have caught up. Some businesses, but far from all, are preparing smart and fast and continuously to protect their business, their people, their property, their data.

Everything you hold digitally in your business is a commodity in the eyes of a cybercriminal. It can, in whole or broken into parts, be monetized, bought, and sold (and often many times over) somewhere in the world.

$3.86M

Global average total cost of a data breach in 2020

$7.13ᴹ	$150	$8.64ᴹ
Healthcare has the highest industry average cost.	Customer PII data has the highest cost per record.	United States has the highest country average cost.

Source: https://www.ibm.com/security/digital-assets/cost-data-breach-report/#/

Digital Data Travels

Even with the now-common credit card frauds we are periodically victim to, we might hear our financial institution asking us (in our US east coast home) if we are not at this moment spending money on our credit card in Hong Kong or London. If it is digitized, it travels.

The cyber threat actor can be keyboarding from his apartment in Helsinki while laying waste to your Nevada-stored customer database. The nation state team of cyber criminals might be sitting in a warehouse outside of St Petersburg in Russia — seizing and holding for ransom your Johannesburg South Africa corporate network.

Cyber criminals are also nimble — adaptable to evolving circumstances and situations. As I write this, we are still in the throes of the 2020 COVID pandemic disruptions to our economy. In order to stay open for business, many have put their personnel to work remotely in their homes. Cyber criminals have already been finding ways to monetize this pandemic and to breach your business's data by hacking into your employees' less-than-robustly protected home office systems and devices. And again, with your staff scattered around, say, the greater Orlando Florida metro area, remember that your criminal is remote, too — perhaps operating from somewhere on a Greek island or from a penthouse office in Rio de Janeiro Brazil.

$137 thousand

Share of respondents who said remote work would increase the time to identify and contain a data breach

Share of respondents who said remote work would increase the cost of a data breach

Remote work impact on the average cost of a data breach

Source: https://www.ibm.com/security/digital-assets/cost-data-breach-report/#/

Chapter 3

Hackers & Other Cyber Criminals

A S I EXPLAINED IN CHAPTER 2, A *HACKER* IS SIMPLY A person using one or more computers to gain access to data he normally would not have authorization to access.

Hacking is not necessarily done for any malicious purpose, though it most certainly can be. There are fictional and real tales we hear, about the teenage geek in the attic beating at government or corporate firewalls from his keyboard — to see how far he can get in entering a protected system, or just for the fun of putting up red flags for an IT team.

While a hacker can certainly do damage and turn to crime (the Black Hats), we've also heard of the hacker who gets hired onto the Cyber Security team of big organizations or a government agency in a protective or defensive role (the White Hats).

White Hat hacking skills are used to test the defenses of the 'house' system and then plug the holes. White Hat hackers are on your side; they look for vulnerabilities and holes in your cyber environment so you can remediate and better defend your assets. They watch the evolution of cybercrime and cyber hacking tools and tactics to stay ahead of them on your behalf.

Cyber *criminals* on the other hand, the Black Hat hackers, are always on the offensive, taking such skills, tools, and actions to a higher level for intentional malicious and criminal purposes. These are wide ranging, from a desire for revenge against an organization, all the way to highly educated and highly organized profit-seeking digital crime against rich organizations.

CTAs, APTs, TTPs, BGH — What Is All This?

Digital crime is high-profit and low-risk to cyber criminals — at least it is lower risk than face-to-face types of crime for the same amounts of money. Cybercrime is definitely organized crime. But anyone who reads the news headlines knows that cybercrime is not only about monetary gain.

Those of us deep in the weeds of cybersecurity have our own shorthand, as you might guess, for the issues we deal with every day as well as for how we categorize the different cyber criminals active across sectors and business types around the world:

CTA. Cyber Threat Actors. This is a generic-sounding term for a common threat, but CTAs are largely money driven. They are global and in it for the long term. Cyber Threat Actors can be BGH (see below). They may work alone and not ever be part of any organization. They will use a range of TTP's (see also below) to suit their crime. Such criminals typically target data to resell or to hold for ransom.

APT. Advanced Persistent Threats. Nation State Actors are the cyber criminals at the top of this category, but there are others just as well funded and just as unrelenting. That is the key concept: They don't give up; they just change their TTPs.

BGH. Big Game Hunters. This educated group of cyber criminals goes after organizations anywhere in the world capable of paying big money in ransoms. They seize and block the corporation's data (in whole or in part) in exchange for money. Ransoms run from 6 figures to tens of millions of dollars or other exchangeable currency. Potential ransomware victims notably include large corporations who have the two-fold attraction of 1) lots of salable and resalable data and 2) deep pockets to pay large cash ransom amounts.

Nation State Actors. Governments other than your own and their own cybercriminal teams. They use a range of TTP's to perform political, economic, or military espionage in other countries. These nation states encourage this cyber espionage and the country's treasury will fund this level of hacking or cyber spying. Teams intentionally and aggressively target public and private sector networks in view to compromising or modifying, destroying or seizing data and information.

As they have the financial backing and ideological support of a national government, these criminals are persistent in their efforts (APTs). Some of the nation state actors — adversaries of the US and other governments, but also of data-rich large corporate entities and all the way down to private individuals — include Russia, China, Iran, North Korea and Pakistan but there are others you might overlook such as Vietnam or India.

Do they attack other nations but also dissident organizations and individuals of their own country? Yes. But make no mistake: Such targets are an attractive potential victim for them; they are your adversaries in cyberspace.

Insiders. Your own present or past employees, contractors, venture, or supply chain/vendor/service providing partners.

An insider is basically anyone in or who can be legitimately allowed into any part of your system for licit purposes, but who ends up wreaking digital havoc. It can happen intentionally or innocently, but it can happen. Intentional breaches are largely either for financial gain or revenge motivations. Typical TTPs include data exfiltration and privilege misuse/abuse.

Hacktivists. Hackers who are activists. These criminal hackers are individually or organizationally motivated by an ideology or a cause. This includes socially, politically, or ideologically driven hackers who target individual or organizational victims ostensibly to effect change, but often just for the publicity they can garner from a high-profile attack. Hacktivism, too, is criminal behavior.

For a hacktivist, money is not always (perhaps never) the motivation. Defacing websites, shutting down sites or modifying them or controlling them in the background is often done in the name of digital activism when the owners of targeted websites are running contrary to the hacktivists' ideals or when overtly opposing them.

Terrorists. This category is defined and designated by the US Department of State for many reasons, and although terrorists' offensive cyber activity is limited compared to other cyber criminals, their cybercrime is always disruptive or harassing in nature. Such groups do not hesitate to use the dark web for communications with each other and to effect recruitments into their organizations.

There is much more to be said about threat actors and their motivations, but I promised not to get too deep in the weeds. What are the tools of a cybercriminal and how can they gain access to your data assets? We cybersecurity specialists call them TTPs:

TTP. Tactics, Techniques, Procedures. This is a continuously evolving list of a wide and inventive range of ways threat actors can breach your system to steal, modify or block (ransom) your data. They are also called 'cyber tools' and, like much of our digital equipment, are available more readily and more cheaply than ever before for all levels and types of threat actors.

Some TTPs are more typical when the criminal targets individual clients of, for instance, a financial organization. Other TTPs are more prevalent when targeting the organization itself.

TTPs include data exfiltration (theft of your data by an employee or outside threat actor) or privilege misuse by an insider; website defacements; claimed leaks; social engineering; direct compromise; remote access trojans and destructive malware; strategic web compromise campaigns and malware (including mobile) malware; Phishing and Spear-phishing; password attacks; business email compromise scams; botnets; ransomware...

They are continuously evolving, and as promised I will not get into the details of how these tactics work. Become familiar with these concepts, as your chief information and security officer and his team will be using them in high level executive or board meetings with you to discuss issues, program upgrades, etc. Be forewarned: Threat actors are more inventive than you know. Be forearmed, by getting educated by your CISO and protected through a cybersecurity program (which I discuss a few chapters from now.)

Chapter 4

Threat Actors Are Everywhere

W HAT IS THE PROFILE, THE BACKGROUND AND TRAIN-
ing, of a cybercriminal?

First, they are everywhere on the planet. Starting at the top with nation-state actors such as Russia and China, they are motivated by numerous purposes when they send their battalions of hackers out into cyberspace against their enemies:

- Gaining political information, targeting elected and appointed officials' data, government institution data, legal structures and all the data within.

- Performing industrial/infrastructural, natural resources, military, and business espionage.

- Effecting disruptions with disinformation, cyber vandalism and other cyberattacks, destruction of infrastructure.

Nation-state actors have the resources to attack your systems and then adapt to your new defenses and strike again... and again. With such deep pockets, nation states, as the top APT or Advanced Persistent Threat actors, actually educate or school their hackers and cyber criminals from a young age. They identify youth with a strong academic record in math, sciences, and computer sciences — and build hacker schools for them. Thus, they have curious, trained young people that they provide with state-of-the-art equipment and access to develop new TTPs and move forward into hacking new markets for new nefarious purposes.

Major powers do this, but nations such as Brazil — a laggard in a sense but that allowed its students to disregard old tools and jump into the new technology with no preconceived barriers in its own hacker schools — catch up faster than we can even imagine.

Cybercriminal groups like Anonymous have a different profile. Anonymous draws from an international and presumably eclectic population of hackers and activists united against censorship. This is an international hacktivist group with no official leadership, headquarters, or even shared philosophy amongst its thousands of 'Anons'. Broadly speaking, Anons all seem to oppose internet censorship and control. Thus, their actions tend to target governments, organizations, and corporations that they accuse of censorship. The group has been variously labeled as digital Robin Hoods and terrorists. Some of the Anons just want to break things; others are driven by a fierce belief in freedom of expression and exchange, i.e.: anti-censorship.

While all cybercrime is clearly of criminal and illegal nature, the dark web is host to entrepreneurs or organizations 'openly' trading in illegal goods and services. In a real sense, the dark web is also global, everywhere, serving the cybercriminals' needs. They sell spyware on the dark web to jealous husbands and criminal stalkers. They sell hacking services or subcontract the cybertheft of digital data. Products that are illegal on the white and gray markets are bought and sold here by enterprising ecommerce webstore owners.

Corporate-versus-corporate crimes might have nothing to do with nation state threat actors but will be about insider threats, domestic competitor spying and cyber disruption. Likewise, industrial espionage against your business is not being only being performed by the fellow with the visitor badge or that foreign government official getting a tour of your site, but via efforts by your domestic competitors offsite to illicitly acquire your proprietary data.

To round out the general and eclectic profile of a cybercriminal, there are cases (HP, Hewlett Packard, 2007) where leaders of a corporation have initiated spying and hacking on their own personnel and board members to discover leaks of corporate information, corporate trade secrets or R&D and the like. As HP discovered to its public discomfort, it is still illegal even if it is done in your own house; it is still cybercrime.

Cyber Criminal versus Cyber Warrior

If cyber criminals are 'civilians', who are cyber warriors? They are the ones who wage war using information technology. They may or may not be actual soldiers in a nation's military forces.

The term cyber warrior may refer to someone with malicious intent (the attacker you are defending against) or a professional on your side who is working to defend against such attackers.

Just as the police forces of the world find and arrest criminals and put preventative tactics in place to reduce crime, cyber warriors are those who fight cyber criminals and defend systems against breach. Just as the military forces of the world fight their nation state enemies, cyber warriors fight cyber criminals affecting their own nation.

We saw how nation states such as Russia, China and Brazil formally train cyber criminals that will work on behalf of their governments against their foreign enemies. Most nation states today also train cyber warriors to protect their own infrastructure from penetration from the outside. In many cases the white hat hacker is the cyber warrior. In the US, cyber warfare is taken seriously by all branches of our military. There are units in each branch that are trained and active in cyber protection.

Indeed, every major nation on the planet has such military units. These units are typically divided into Blue Teams and Red Teams — as in sports, one plays offense and the other is defensive. The Red teams are offensive security experts, attacking systems and breaking into defenses, or least attempting to do so. Blue teams are the defensive units who work to build and enhance internal network defenses against successful attacks and threats by the Reds. Much like wargames, Blue and Red teams vie against each other to up their games, enhance all protections and understand all types of breaches and threats for the good of the organization.

Perhaps the most publicized inter-nation case (US/Israel/Iran) of cyber warfare involves the Stuxnet cyberweapon. 'Stuxnet' is a worm that is ostensibly responsible doing damage to prevent Iranian nuclear development. Neither nation has admitted to it; however, the US and Israel were the purported offensive cyber warriors defending their respective national interests by creating and inserting the Stuxnet worm into the Iranian systems.

Other Threat Actors

Cyberterrorists are state sponsored but also non-state threat actors who engage in cyberattacks for their own criminal, idealistic, disruptive and profit seeking motives. There is not always a clear-cut distinction between cyber spies and cyber terrorists (both are cybercriminals), except perhaps by examining their targets or the havoc they have wreaked. Likewise, it is not always obvious whether a cyberattack is criminal, an act of hacktivism, domestic or international terrorism, or a nation-state's cyber warfare against another sovereign state. When your corporation is also a government or military contractor these lines blur, but your Cyber Security Program (and more on this in a coming chapter) must evolve to remain a true barrier between your organization and skilled cybercriminals. Your vigilance must clearly be continuous.

You might believe that it is unlikely that cyberterrorism per se will affect your corporation or organization, but again, forewarned is forearmed. Getting a sense of "what a cybercriminal looks like" can arm you, erase some of your naiveté about who the aggressors might be and help you defend against them.

Stuxnet

"I think we're living in the world of non-response. Where you know that there's a problem, but you don't do anything about it. If that's denial, then that's denial."

—RICHARD CLARKE

The Stuxnet Incident at the Iranian Natanz Enrichment Plant

STUXNET IS A DIGITAL WORM. IT IS MALWARE THAT REPlicates itself spreading copies to other computers without any human interaction. It was such a worm that was used to cause failure in centrifuges — essentially ruin them — in the Iranian enrichment plant, Natanz.

Stuxnet is commonly credited as the first digital weapon introduced and first to attack a SCADA (supervisory control and data acquisition) system. A SCADA system is made up of hardware and software components used to monitor and control industrial processes. SCADA systems are common in industries such as energy, oil and gas refining, transportation, telecommunications, and water and waste plants.

On the surface, you might say worms are created by the thousands a day. Stuxnet, which is a must-read absolutely fascinating story, wasn't out to steal data, which is a common objective. Rather, its purpose was to cause the physical annihilation of machinery being operated by computing systems controlling the machinery. When you think about its purpose, to halt or slow Iran from developing nuclear weapons by destroying centrifuges used to enrich uranium, the Stuxnet tale becomes even more captivating; there were ways that utilize conventional weapons that could have stopped the enrichment process.

If you don't know the story or recall it, it is worth mentioning the actors involved. Obviously, Iran, and Israel and the United States are commonly known as the collaborators that worked on creating Stuxnet.

Although at the time, Israel, as is their modus operandi, did not come out and state they were involved, a video at Lieutenant Genera Gabi Ashkenazi's retirement party in 2011 listed Stuxnet as one of his operational successes. General Ashkenazi headed IDF (Israel Defense Forces) from February 2007 to February 2011.

The US involvement was first authorized by President George W. Bush to create a digital map of Natanz. Obama took over the program dubbed "Olympic Games". In 2010, Stuxnet, which was never intended, leaked out of Natanz. During a briefing with President Obama and Vice President Biden, it was speculated that the leak occurred due to someone's laptop connecting to the internet. Stuxnet, doing what Stuxnet is supposed to do, spread.

A coding error was blamed, and a blame game ensued; Biden was heard to state, "It's got to be the Israelis".

This story is intriguing on many fronts. One, and mentioned above, it is known as the first digital weapon used by one nation against another — a state against state attack. Also, the design aspects are intriguing, from what went into the architecture to the deployment method.

Years in the making and launching in 2009 or so, there was collaboration between many groups and two countries, crossing US Presidential administrations during its planning, development, and deployment by utilizing a USB stick to compromise the systems due to the facility being air-gapped (unable to communicate via the internet outside facility walls).

Another intriguing aspect is that at the time (mid to late 2000s) and upon its discovery in 2010, cybersecurity defense tools and cyber security programs were not sophisticated. At the time of discovery, Stuxnet made a statement.

Henceforth, no nation needs conventional weapons to accomplish security or aggression objectives. We have the capability to turn the lights out on any country with the sophisticated digital weapons we already possess.

I love the Stuxnet story for many reasons, but primarily because of the collaboration that took place as well as its peaceful nature — nobody died, nobody got hurt. It is like a ghost showed up and destroyed the facility, then vanished without a trace. It was the stuff of spy action movies!

Through the security analysis done subsequently, we now know there were traces. These few words cannot do the Stuxnet story justice, but if I have intrigued you a bit I highly recommend reading the book *Countdown to Zero Day: Stuxnet and the Launch of the World's First Digital Weapon,* by Kim Zetter; it is a truly fascinating and detailed account of Stuxnet.

There is another 'mystery' of what potentially could be called the first weapon used against a nation state. It is the story of the CIA and Siberian Pipeline explosion in 1982. The explosion supposedly measure 1/7 that of the nuclear weapons dropped on Japan in World War II and vaporized part of the pipeline.

How did it happen? It has been reported that a Colonel who served as a head of the KGB Directorate sent the French intelligence information containing Soviet classified documents; these documents turned out to be very useful. In the documents were names of Soviet Agents tasked with stealing western technology. The files were shared between the French and US Presidents. The Soviets wanted technology to better run their Siberian pipeline. For operations of the sophisticated control systems, they needed software and had approached the US for the software; the US turned them down. The Soviets depended on the US and Western technology to drill more difficult deposits. A KGB agent then turned to a Canadian supplier, but the US tipped off the supplier. The Canadians "improved" the software. After a lapse amount of time (think logic bomb), the software reset pump speeds and other settings then ... BANG!

You noted the dates Stuxnet was developed in the mid-2000s, with the attack launching somewhere around 2009, and all damage being fully discovered only in 2010. If that hasn't quite registered as an "OMG!" moment, then let me clarify my thought when I see that timeframe. At the time I write this it is September 2020; over 10 years has passed. Imagine the many *more* countries that have become capable of this type of activity in the past decade. Imagine what the US, Israel, other superpowers like

Russia, China, and the UK are capable of doing. For this reason alone (though there are countless others), it is my belief that we are at the dawn of our Coming Cyber War.

PART TWO

Business Executives

I N THESE NEXT CHAPTERS, I PRESENT SOME ADVICE ABOUT your in-house cyber security to guide C-suite executives or executives in C-suite roles. Indeed, this advice is for all leaders of businesses of any size and operating in any industry or economic sector.

Cyber threat actors don't care what industry you are in. All they are interested in is whether they can hack your data for their own profit or for other motives they might be pursuing, such as pure disruption or some political ideal. For threat actors, "it's not personal, it's just business" every hour of every day, and so it must be for you as well.

Your job is to bring your strong leadership skills and all-encompassing understanding of business fundamentals to the game of protecting your organization from these threats — remembering that they might be coming from within your own walls. Perhaps it is a new responsibility for you to be on "cyber watch", but it is a new line item in your job description that will not go away.

COOs, CMOs and CFOs and others of you are going to have operational aspects of the business as your purview. You each need to learn to empower your team or division by empowering and interacting strategically with a CISO (Chief Information Security Officer). Your first best step is acknowledging that your cybersecurity, information security, and information technology teams are not just "the guys in the basement". That ship has sailed!

In our 21st century, you need to move your information team out of the basement and out of the server room and into the executive suite. You need a highly knowledgeable, experienced CISO and he or she needs to be in the executive suite and in your board room with you. Likewise, your technology team's needs — no matter what business you are in — must henceforth be given an honorable place in your annual budgets, as they are facing new threats every month, and will need the new tools that they or other professionals have developed to combat them.

It is time to make a strategic and concerted effort to mature your own knowledge of cyber security and cyber threats, and not only shift into using your data more effectively, but also into the development of your business's strategic and actionable cyber defensive program.

Chapter 5

Data Is The New Gold

DATA IS KING IN BUSINESS, THE NEW GOLD. IT IS MULTI-faceted and we give it various names. It might be IP; privacy data (medical, financial, credit card, etc.); inventory data; marketing and sales' customer lists; R&D designs, prototypes, notes and logs; business intelligence (KPI tracking, reporting, benchmarking, etc.); video and audio recordings of meetings (authorized and illicit); employee personal data (Social Security and banking information, address and health information, performance reviews, background check results); data from your labs, clean rooms, R&D work spaces and factory floors...

What else qualifies as "a data asset"? Tweets, social media posts, web browser history, the fitness tracker you wear when you jog every morning, any ATM transaction you perform (any FinTech usage), any app you download and use on your smart phone, information from your automobile's GPS, the point of sale system in the restaurant or café you had lunch at (FinTech again), the camera feeds in your surveillance system, and the digital tracking tools used in healthcare to measure bed availability and (today in 2020) numbers of pandemic patients and their symptoms/ treatments...

Government and mega-corporations obviously use data, but so do the solopreneurs running a lucrative eCommerce business or two from their kitchen table.

Some companies exist only because of data. Equifax is a prime example. It is a credit bureau. Credit bureaus are data collectors. Data is "what they do". The big breach at Equifax was about cyber criminals wanting to get the data on every individual in the Equifax databases and they pretty much succeeded. The hackers could then... sell and resell that data; use it themselves for personal enrichment through isolated Identity Theft sting operations; stalk individuals for harassment value; ransom the data of individuals who looked like "a good payment bet" and more. Up and down the hierarchy and across functions, Equifax (if that had not already been the case) was brutally and suddenly awakened to the fact that:

1) data is the whole company's responsibility and

2) data collection and protection was in fact the only 'raison d'être' of the company.

On top of it all, they made headline news and could no longer keep their head down vis-à-vis consumers and consumer watchdog groups nor keep their heads in the sand about their protective responsibilities.

Some companies take risks by not knowing the value of the data they possess. An example is an established defense contractor that periodically removed older formerly sensitive digitized files from protected status into an 'archive' status. When that older data (still valuable, and even at that late date absolutely still monetizable by hackers) started appearing in non-company publications and under discussion in meetings in and outside the company, their federal contacts got wind of it. C-suite realized the archive was unprotected (and that their CIO knew it) and raced to close the breach after the damage was done. They also moved to review the business's cyber protection needs in relation to the technical personnel they employed, and made serious upgrades there, too.

Digitization will continue to produce vast amounts of data, and the responsibility of which types of data you collect, use, work with and hold must henceforth be a matter of centrally determined C-suite strategy that is passed down to the functional teams and staff. It is you who will be mapping your data's path, and prioritizing its location, access, and protections.

I could go on and on. The types and volumes of Big Data are growing so fast that in its *Cisco's Visual Networking Index: Forecast and Methodology 2016-2021*, Cisco forecast that "global Internet traffic in 2021 will be equivalent to 127 times the volume of the entire global Internet in 2005."

Evaluating that Gold

For a long time now in the best protected businesses, your business's data has not been the sole responsibility of your IT division or team. Managers across the business have taken some share of responsibility, perhaps in a decentralized way. That is why C-suite must be more hands-on, knowledgeable, informed than before. Your company-wide data is hackable (everything is), monetizable (everything is), available to threat actors (of all profile types). Not protecting your data is putting your business and your people at risk.

Never assume you know the "shelf life" of your data nor its value to a cybercriminal. From its creation to archiving it years down the road, to ensuring that data is appropriately interpreted and converted into insight — inform yourself on the flow and evolution of your business data. Know its nature, where it is, who has access to it and why, and what they are doing with it.

So-called old data may have a real value for your business beyond what you have thought about. But it also may have value to another nation state putting together "profiles" or historic behavioral materials about our nation or your industry. Your historic data paints a picture, shows some statistical valuable trends, demonstrates agility or blocks in the marketplace and more — to those looking for such saleable tidbits. Don't assume you know the monetizable value of your data outside your business.

Know this: Cyber thieves think quite differently about its value and who might buy it from them than you do; you need to get into their heads and protect all your data.

84% of the S&P 500's value is constituted by intangible assets: Data. Your company is probably no different. Your business has value in such a large part due to the data you generate, analyze, and hold that you must protect it all. Big data is astonishing quick and easy to collect. Knowing what to do with it and how to benefit from it within your business is another matter. 80% of worldwide "data assets" is privately held by businesses. You are making money from it. Protect it.

It is no secret that the five most valuable companies in the world are Big Data giants Apple, Amazon, Facebook, Microsoft, and Alphabet (Google). They live and breathe data and make big money doing so. "Amazon now captures 46% of online shopping" in America, while Google and Facebook "accounted for about 99% of the $2.9 billion" growth in digital advertising in 2016, according to *How Google and Facebook Have Taken Over The Digital Ad Industry*, (Fortune magazine article by Matthew Ingram, January 4, 2017).

My guess is that these players are also our current masters of connecting all that disparate global data to arrive at the answers they need to grow their businesses, crush competition, improve the bottom line and all sorts of internal efficiencies and foresee where the market is going before anyone else does. Yet International Data Corporation (IDC) projects that more than 85% of Fortune 500 organizations will fail to exploit Big Data for competitive advantage; there is too much of it to wrap that thinking around. I don't believe our large corporations are that masterful, yet, with their Big Data, and therein lies another way we need to think about data. How do we weave it all together to arrive at useful, effective conclusions that are also true…all the while protecting it as the gold mine it is for our businesses?

According to Gartner, the volume of information is growing at an annual rate of 59% globally. Google already processed 600 petabytes of data monthly by 2012, with the number of businesses storing 1 petabyte of data (a million gigabytes) also increasing exponentially.

Few companies are prepared such a continuous flood of data. This amount of data is more than just "big". The more data your business must store, the more complex your systems (people, infrastructure, access controls, analysis of data) and their protection become. Your job is to know that and how you are up to the task.

The value of your data must never be underestimated, no matter what your past management approach has been. Threat actors don't misjudge its value. Data is the currency being traded on the Dark Web like a currency — sold and bought over and over again under it is wrung dry. It is like gold — and to a threat actor, more valued than gold. That valuable, crucial data you have at your company is the crown jewel.

Your data is not the PowerPoint slide showing the 2nd floor Café buildout! You could not lose your company or be locked out of your databases or lose a day's revenues if it went astray. I nonetheless encourage you to be overly encompassing when you define "data", and as you measure and categorize the data you hold and need to protect. You need to be as creative in thinking about and defining your valuable data as the threat actor who steals it from you. Like a jeweler working with a lump of gold, and who can turn it into all manner of valued and pricey objects from jewelry to industrial parts, you too must now "think like a creative crook" when you and your fellow executives analyze which of your data needs better protection. Your data has a wide range of value that cyber criminals can turn it into and monetize. Think like them and start protecting it.

A case in point of the type of data, companies might fail to protect because of misperception of its resaleable (by threat actors) potential: The engineered design of a car door. It seems mundane and of little value or interest? Wrong! It is important if you are a vehicle manufacturer. It is part of your Intellectual Property. The door on an American name-brand sedan which I will not name is the same door now being assembled on a Chinese car… This is an example of IP stolen from American companies by Chinese industrial spies. Will it break the US company or set it back? Only C-suite strategic thinking can answer such a question.

Another case in point is my own region's industry. I'm in the gas/oil hub of Houston Texas. Here corporations of the industry need to combat threats from around the world. Industrial espionage is performed and contracted by international competing companies. Cyber espionage is contracted by nation states at the highest levels of governance when the nation has with oil and gas interests to protect. Stolen data can cost such corporations billions of dollars. There is vibrant competition domestically, so they can never assume that "Americans protect American interests" is going to hold true. There is much talent movement amongst corporations in the industry as well, so each business needs stiff confidentiality controls in place as regards data protection.

Like the oil and gas industry, you must likewise protect your data from both international and domestic interference by your competitors whatever your activity. You might be underbid by one or more competitors who stole your bid data before submitting their own. How much one or more lost contracts might cost your company is another matter to resolve at a C-suite strategic level.

As a last example for now, consider the data your marketing team is collecting. It allows, as one instance, your teams to pinpoint with greater accuracy which silo of customer is best served by which of your products and to go out and find more new customers like them. Your customer preference data is thus also valuable to your direct and indirect competitors who might hack it themselves — or hire out the hack. Protect it. Protect your legitimate, hard-earned edge in the marketplace.

Cyber criminals and threat actors are not the only ones collecting and monetizing your data. Don't forget that top five most valuable companies on the planet are doing a fine job of collecting all sorts of "permissioned" data from you and reselling it (to marketers and pollsters) ... quite licitly. Don't give away your data (whether you, like the Big 5, monetize it yourself or not) through lack of protections.

Personnel You Need

Europeans are legislating data through The *General Data Protection Regulation* (*GDPR*), which is a legal framework in place since 2019 setting guidelines for the collection and processing of personal information from individuals who live in the European Union.

Back home, federal and state lawmakers in the US have a hard time deciding the basic question of whether data is private property or not.

Even though the US has no encompassing legislation at this time, business is global, and you will be subject the GDPR and other nations' laws when you do business there. Does your organization need an attorney on tap who understands the international intricacies of cyber security issues, an attorney who will track regulations in the making and make sense of legislation currently being enforced? Perhaps.

There is certainly somewhat of a digital divide between the top 5 technology/data giants alongside our mega-corporations and our smaller corporations and businesses. Cyber security is a business-wide concern reaching now into the executive suite of all businesses, of all sizes, in all sectors. Do not fail to understand how closely the very existence of your business depends on data and your unfettered access to it. Do not underestimate the speed at which the threat environment can and will evolve.

In C-suite, your job is to balance the risk of data breaches (including total loss, sabotaged or compromised data, locked or ransomed data) with how to keep operating on a daily basis without too-strict controls over the flow of that data. Your people need access to your data to a greater or less or extent in order to remain responsive, relevant, and competitive in your customers' and partners' eyes.

Chapter 6

Waking Up to See Yourself on the Front Page of *The Wall Street Journal*

IN MARCH 2020, MARRIOTT INTERNATIONAL INC., HEAD-quartered in Bethesda Maryland, had a breach. The threat actors ended up capturing 5.2 million customers' personal information. This was not a first for the corporation; two other cyber incidents made this the third breach in 18 months. What exactly is "customers' personal information"? What was stolen included guests' names, addresses, birthdays, emails, phone numbers and loyalty reward program numbers for both the hotel chain and partner airlines. How did the hackers get it? The data was accessed using login credentials of two employees of a franchised Marriott Hotel in Russia.

Back to Equifax, which I brought up in the prior section. Their breach crisis claimed the job of Richard Smith, the Chief Executive Officer. The attackers had accessed dozens of sensitive databases and created more than 30 separate entry points into

Equifax's computer systems by the time the breach was discovered and dealt with. That is lots of "open doors" for threat actors to waltz through…

There was also some evidence in the Equifax investigation that the initial hackers handed off the access to a more highly skilled team; investigators suspect a nation-state was behind the hack. Some insist it was Chinese intelligence, but there is no conclusive evidence identifying Chinese threat actors. This said, investigators found similarities to breaches in a healthcare business (Anthem) and a US government unit (Office of Personnel Management). Be aware that though threat actors may specialize as individuals, organizations go where the data wealth lies.

The Equifax breach demonstrates the high risk that remains even if your business, like Equifax had, has spent millions on cyber security and employs in-house security personnel (the company ran a dedicated operations center and deployed a suite of expensive anti-intrusion software; they alas also suffered poor implementation and the departure of key personnel). It also demonstrates how hard it can be to clearly identify the threat actor behind any incident.

California-based First American Financial Corp is a leading provider of title insurance and settlement services for the real estate and mortgage industries. It employs 18,000 people and brought in more than $5.7 billion in 2018. Yet, in May 2019, the Web site for this Fortune company leaked hundreds of millions of documents related to mortgage deals going back to 2003. The digitized records included records of wire transactions with bank account numbers and bank statements, mortgage and tax records, Social Security numbers, driver license images of buyer/seller clients. It appeared that all the data was available without authentication to anyone with a Web browser.

The First American breach of spring 2020 was one of the biggest since Yahoo's massive incident in 2013 that lost data on three billion accounts.

The First American breach quickly surpassed a prior data breach which has since been named "Collection #1" — for the most records breached in 2019. The overall database "collection" represents over 773 million unique email addresses and 21 million unique passwords, which provide more than 2.7 billion email/password pairs. This theft of email addresses and passwords appeared on the Dark Web in January 2019. The list contains exposed addresses and passwords from over 2000 previous data breaches as well as an estimated 140 million new email addresses and 10 million new passwords from unknown sources. It is thus not the booty from one breach, but from many.

These are just a tiny taste of the stories — the companies, the executives — of breaches that made headline news. These stories were gobbled up by online newsfeeds and broadcast far and wide to all types of readership, worldwide.

Do you really want to have your name in lights in this way?

The New York State Department of Financial Services and the California Consumer Privacy Act (CCPA) and California's Attorney General are two of the first US states developing robust cyber security laws in view to protecting citizens' data held in US companies. Both got involved in the First American case (California's CCPA is fining American Title $200M), which spilled lots of ink on blogs and print news media. Whether or not your business is active in the state of California or in New York, heads up. There are consequences to not buttoning down your data.

Don't Be the Breaking News

Do you really want to be Breaking News on tonight's 6pm broadcast, or have your picture plastered on the front page of the WSJ? As a business executive, you cannot shirk the responsibilities you have for cyber security. You can no longer pass them off to the IT department and expect them to "take care of it". Those days are gone, if they ever existed. It is also no longer the purview of a single executive even if that person is your company's CISO or CTO. You likewise cannot expect your legal team, even with a cybersecurity attorney on board, to have its finger on the pulse of your data security.

It is, from now on, an all-hands-on-deck obligation of stewardship. All executives, whatever their operational purview, have a responsibility to the company to empower a strong Cyber Security Program.

Today if you are breached, you'll end up on the front page of the WSJ, plastered all over online and cable headline news, slammed (mocked, reviled ... imagine the worst) on social and in professional digital media. When I say "you", I mean your business. But I also mean "you" the single corporate executive that you are. There have been no small number of high-profile breaches of data in which C-suite executives have gone to jail or had ruined reputations. This may happen to you perhaps as its leader, but certainly the company name will be tossed about with malicious glee. To make things more painful, there are the fines that the courts levy and that your business must pay. It is hard to budget time, energy, lost reputation, and money as a result of a class-action lawsuit (and those fines of millions of dollars that result). You cannot shirk or pass off this cyber security responsibility.

Chapter 7

Not Just Your Reputation
or Raw Data at Stake

IN THE PRECEDING CHAPTER, WE DISCUSSED YOUR OWN reputation in the event of a cyber breach. In North America, around 32% or one-third of all data breaches resulted in a C-level executive, president or even CEO of a company losing that job due to the effects of the breach. Kaspersky Labs studied the matter and based this statement on 5,878 interviews with businesses of all sizes from 29 countries. I must repeat: Businesses of all sizes and in all sectors and activities and anywhere in the world are at risk.

While it is true that your own reputation as a business executive could take a hit through a cyberattack that happened on your watch, it is not just about you.

While it is true that your data is at stake, it is not just about your business's raw data, either.

Your company could go bankrupt in very short order. Your company could close entirely due to cyberattacks. Think of ransomware attacks that your business could never afford to pay, and that the data held hostage prevents business operations of any kind. Ransoms lock up your strategic, financial, and operational information and perhaps the ability to run your businesses, infrastructure, plants, and other entities. Think of the cost of repairing damage done by hackers to your data banks and your infrastructure that your business can also not really afford while ensuring any kind of business continuity.

You might have high-dollar liabilities such as a ransomware. You might have unbudgeted and unaffordable cyber-remedy/repair costs.

Imagine the jobs lost. The lost trust. Data breaches in too great a number and announced or dealt with in a too-public clumsy manner (such as initial denial that you later backpedal away from) could erase all the goodwill with customers and other company partners to the degree that business as you knew it is lost for good.

A cyberattack might not affect your business alone, as you are linked to vendors and others in your internet-connected supply chain or linked to all manner of economically connected businesses and individuals. In other words, the attack on your business can have a hacker-designed ripple effect out to all those digitally connected to the business in any way.

In 2019, there 811 breaches registered in the US with the Identity Theft Resource Center, collectively affecting 493 million individuals. Read that again, where the key word is "registered". Each breach is said to cost $3.86M to the breached businesses. We are halfway through 2020 at this writing, and there have been 540 breaches affecting 163.5 million individuals.

In the case of a breach of any type or of any proportion, it is not only your company reputation and continuity, but all executives' reputations, personnel livelihoods, and economically connected partners risk serious disruption. When customers and your own personnel lose faith in your abilities to protect their data and have lost trust that you will ever be proactive, what level of business do you have left?

Be clear: The most difficult and costly consequences of a cyberattack to remedy and recover are loss of your IP (in the #1 spot, and many such breaches go undetected for years), loss of strategic information, loss of reputation, a higher cost of capital (including loss of value on the financial markets, as investors are paying attention), loss or modifications of data. At the end of the day, a breach reaches further than the apparent harm you initially identify.

Perhaps your business is quite large and has deep pockets, so you don't feel the financial urgency of advanced cybersecurity. After all, the statistics we are collating show that 43% of all cyberattacks target small businesses, and that 60% of small companies go out of business within six months of a data breach or cyberattack. Small business risk includes business banking accounts being hacked and the most recently measured average loss is $32,000 — quite a lot of ready cash to disappear for any independent small business.

The other 57% of attacks are directed at businesses just like yours. Whether you have 10 or 10,000 employees, the world is becoming increasingly connected, and the number, size and effects of data breaches is rising — and fast. Don't get smug because you are an executive in a billion+ dollar business with deep pockets. Don't get smug because you believe hackers have no interest in your industry, much less your "little, tiny" business. Instead, pause and consider your organization's own willingness and ability to "pay up". Consider the effects of a major hack of any of your most coveted data bases, IP (trade secrets, unpatented inventions, and others). Because make no mistake, the richer your company is or is perceived to be *in resalable data whatever its nature*, the higher the ransom to get your data back and the higher the repair price tag when the dust settles.

Again, this warning applies absolutely to mega-corporations with international reach, but also to $10M regional companies that can't afford the $500,000 ransom. You believe that your $100B corporation could survive but consider the total cost.

Risks to Your Consumers

It is not just "raw data" you own that is at risk. It is not just your business continuity at risk, either. You should be alarmed by the extent and types of cyber risks you create "by design" for your consumers. Depending on your industry, your tech-built and tech-driven product lines are at high risk and not just from corporate espionage like the Chinese stealing the digital blueprints of your newly engineered car door.

Case in point: If you are in life-supporting products as so many are within the medical industry, and one of your "medical devices" got hacked — lives are at stake. Why? Theft is not the only motivation for hackers. Competitors and nation states are just as gleeful to modify your design in a tiny, lethal way for the destruction of your reputation. They would love to see you in the courts of law defending an indefensible design, while in some plant across the globe they are producing your original safe-and-effective design. This is not a fictional or futuristic case: The FDA is warning patients, medical providers and hospitals that software susceptibilities might allow a hacker to take control of devices connecting to wireless networks such as pacemakers and infusion pumps; hackers can also use such devices to locate a "back door" into entire hospital networks. Could your pacemaker kill with a small malicious tweak to its design?

Similarly, in April 2020, Interpol warned that cyber criminals are using ransomware to target healthcare organizations — and especially those already overwhelmed (and distracted) by COVID-19. Interpol also noted an increase in identified health system attacks since the start of the pandemic, with ransoms holding patient record access hostage until the ransom is paid. Could your heart monitors fail due to a malicious data modification? If you are a health industry business, this is not a sci-fi movie but your very existence that is at stake; it is real people whose lives are at stake. Will your patients and community ever trust you again?

Any business using increased digital or tele-service or remotely-accessible service to alleviate the stresses of doing businesses during COVID shutdowns — beware. You have just increased the bandwidth of access for cyber criminals.

Here is another case in point: All Internet-of-Things devices and other tech-driven products. All of them are at-risk devices firstly by the very fact of connection to the internet and secondly, they are not designed/manufactured with any built-in safeguards. 98% of all IoT data traffic is not encrypted; thus, even a so-called medium level cyberattack could compromise them.

Look at the current development of self-driving cars. As traditionally driven by humans, vehicles of any type are already recognized as weapons in the wrong driver's hands. That leads you to consider the weaponization potential of a tech-driven vehicle when the software is tweaked by a maliciously intentioned hacker. It's your products running on tech and not just clients' personal financial/health data or information that is at risk.

These two cases alone demonstrate the risks you bring to

your consumers when you are not building products that include cyber defenses.

Your business may produce consumer-targeted IoT products: smart refrigerators, smart watches, smart fire alarm, smart door lock, smart bicycle, medical sensors, fitness trackers, smart security system (security system captures video and audio and sends data over the internet to your smart phone), smart doorbells, smart locks, smart speakers, switches, cameras...

Your business certainly uses IoT devices to help you run operations, such as sensors and systems for detecting oil/gas spills and increasing safety; GPS tracking for monitoring corporate fleets (assets and vehicles); RFID tags and other technology for asset tracking... and the list is long.

Cisco believes there are now over 20 billion "smart devices" globally — devices that are embedded with technology such as processing chips, software, and sensors. Embedded with the goal of collecting data and sharing it with other devices and systems over the hackable internet.

Cyber Security—At What Price?

As a cyber security officer, myself, I have noted how many corporations are unwilling to spend the money it takes for a robust cyber security program. I believe the deeper reason for backing away from a high performance, evolving cyber security program is the false belief that such measures slow down company operations on an individual employee level but also on an overall corporate flow level. This is inaccurate. No driver would say that the brakes of his vehicle keep him from maintaining highway speed on an open road. Cyber security measures, like the brake pedal, are there for protection when the need arises and if implemented collaboratively should not interrupt the smooth flow of business operations, but rather create and/or add to efficiencies. It is a system of defenses that operate invisibly to the employee and customer, humming and alert in the background of your daily operations.

Fully half of CIOs and CTOs are hands-off in cyber security matters. That is what my earlier story about the defense company was about: They had discovered, as other corporations have, that their CIO and/or CTO were not only unschooled but uninvolved in implementing cyber security measures needed by the organization. Being "compliant" is no longer enough, as has not been enough for a long time. Being "all systems go" operationally is also not enough and never will be again.

The price of not hiring an educated, fully informed, continuously trained and engaged CISO can knock your business right out of the marketplace. While corporations have employed CSOs — Chief Security Officers — in their executive suites for a while, that executive was initially concerned with the physical security of your organization, not just the cyber security of it; the role evolved to include cyber and the roles were eventually split. Enter the CISO, who is the Information (read: digital data) Security Officer, and you now invest in two levels of security for your organization. You will often times see the physical security executive as a Director/VP of Corporate Security.

But even as a non-technical executive yourself, you must not be hands-off. I will never stop stating this. You cannot abdicate your responsibilities in this domain. Once word gets out on the street that you were at the helm during a cyber breach crisis, other job opportunities you might have had are likely to dissolve.

As the IBM chart below shows us, too many CEOs but also COOs, CFOs and (I hate to say it, but there you are) CIOs act like cybersecurity is "someone else's job". If you value your business, its growth, its relevance, and longevity in the marketplace ... if you value your own professional and personal reputation and future employability ... get involved in your business's cyber security. Future employability? Yes. Cyber security knowledge is a transferable skill. It is learnable for the non-technical executives. Those executives with such transferable knowledge will always be in demand in our Big Data future.

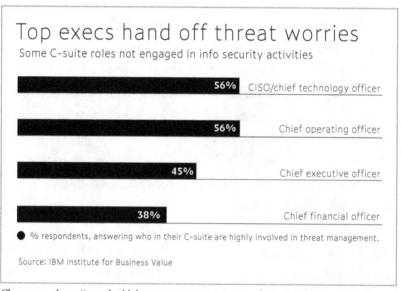

Chart source: https://www.healthdatamanagement.com/opinion/how-to-make-an-effective-case-for-increasing-the-security-budget

Chapter 8

Are You in Charge or is Your CISO?

A T THE START OF THIS MILLENNIUM, FEW BUSINESSES of any consequential size specifically employed a CISO whose domain was purely digital security (as opposed to the very common "physical" security officer or CSO that all large businesses employed and as opposed to the purely technology and networking functions filled by a CTO). Today, businesses worth over $3B in revenue and many doing over $300M have a recognized head of information security, or CISO. The digital sea that corporations had been swimming in for a number of years suddenly came to C-suite and Board room attention as an area that demanded risk protections. The physical security team was not up to the task, nor (as it soon became painfully clear) were the directors of IT and their teams.

If C-suite was not in charge — and it wasn't because of the lack of cyber expertise — and the CSO and CTO were not in charge — and they were not because they did lack that specific training…who was it going to be that identified and mitigated the growing cyber risks of the business?

Now that you have engaged a CISO for that role in your business, I must repeat the question: Are you in charge or is it the CISO? Who is in charge of the CISO? Who reports to the CISO? Have you empowered your CISO with the right structure? This is important in the cyber security field because strategy and policy must be decided at the top and security needs continuity across all teams. Implicit is that knowledge about cyber security threats and needs also resides with the top executive in charge. Again, is the top exec in charge the CISO or …?

Although today the functions of CSO and CISO are necessarily interlocked, ensuring cyber security is different from safeguarding your physical plant, people, and facilities (the CSO's purview). It is about the digitized information you collect and store. About robust access controls to the data, so that you know who is authorized to be in the systems and which part of the data that authorizes. It is about how and who navigates with your data in cyber spaces, by controlling the devices and applications used.

If you are in direct charge and you don't have your finger on the pulse of data, risks escalate, and you lose all semblance of control. Cyber threats evolve hourly, and that is the attention your systems need from you. If you have a CISO, and have hired him wisely, trust him and his team to do the job without micromanaging or constraining them on budgets.

What Exactly Is a CISO?

Your Chief Information Security Officer is the primary executive responsible for devising your cyber security strategy that will ensure that all your information/data assets are truly protected in an evolving way. This officer is up to date on regulatory and compliance matters imposed upon your business from the outside as well as policies and procedures decided from within the business. A CISO is schooled and skilled at-risk assessment and with defining policies and procedures associated with eliminating or mitigating risks.

This executive is the key touchpoint for all cyber incidents (discovery of malware and hacking, insider vandalism, etc.). He is the primary leader in any cyber crisis — dealing with repairing the breach, certainly, but also directing recovery from its consequences to and within the organization.

He and his teams are your architect for the systems and processes that keep your data secure. This officer is the key, technical individual with business acumen in your business keeping up to date on cyber threats and the types of cyber defenses you need. He is one of the executive officers who can be deep in the weeds of what every division, department, and team of your company is doing operationally and how cyber-safe everyone is keeping themselves.

Given the scope of the position; potential costs to the organization of breaches and failures; and the complexity, time, energy, monetary cost of breaches, preventative measures, post-breach repairs and operational recovery — I hope I have painted a picture of a highly stressful executive position which you need to fill wisely for your organization. A CISO will ideally be the calm eye in the storm of cyber threats and breaches and losses (however temporary) to your organization.

The CISO makes recommendations to the other executives and also to the business's board of directors. By having access to and full awareness of all the businesses external partners this officer allows the business to stay one step ahead of breaches in partner businesses and all manner of threats sourced in those vendor businesses that may affect your own.

Henceforth (if that is not already the case in your business), the CISO sits right on the top line of your organizational chart, should be empowered, and fully supported for them to succeed.

Not in Isolation

The CISO can no more work in isolation than can your CMO or your CFO. If your business is large enough to have a CIO/CTO, a chief information officer/chief technology officer (some larger organizations may have both), as well as a CSO, a chief security officer, these three executives will be needing to work in tandem on a daily basis in clearly differentiated but synergistic functions, while also working as a team with all the other executives of the organization. Clearly defined functions will prevent each of these teams from overlapping efforts, double spending money, doubling up on process creation and generally doing each other's jobs instead of their own.

The CISO should likewise be working with each of your other company executives on a frequent, regular basis to protect each of their business units and build out their protection program in collaboration with one another.

As in many areas that are unknown to us and make us fearful, education in cyber security and cyber threats (and how to detect them in real time) only makes sense as your company training program's #1 priority. Your CISO thus also wears a hat as your CCE, or Chief Cyber Educator for all employees working in your business. As such, the CISO must be supported in his own continuing education (studying with the highest quality educational organizations in the field; participating in industry conferences and the like) as the cyber threat landscape is rich, ever-evolving and needs this officer and his team(s) to be in a state-of-the-minute awareness of threats, remedies and further preventative solutions.

A Full-Fledged Executive Committee Member

The CISO is a C-suite executive and must participate in all executive meetings and committees. The CISO is right on the top line of your security organizational chart, and shoulder-to-shoulder with all other C-suite executives. If the CFO doesn't want to learn about marketing, she depends on the CMO's input at executive meetings. The CISO is your resident master of all things cyber security, cyber risk and cyber defenses, and if you don't want to learn any of the details of his specialization, you'll need to depend on his input on virtually a daily basis.

You would not hire a CFO and put her in an office to do only Accounts Receivable. In the same way, your CISO is an empowered, enabled business partner whom you consult and collaborate with daily. While it is true that your cybersecurity defenses protect you silently in the background of your business operations, your CISO needs to be actively consulted, participate in all executive meetings whatever the topic, and be consulted in new cyber security needs whenever a strategic new direction is decided or new tools adopted.

A CISO is regularly called to board of directors' meetings to make recommendations, report on progress of various programs approved and in place, and to keep their fingers on the pulse of the organization's security measures. Other executives in the C-suite must accept that this is a vital part of business continuity, and request reports from the CISO at their own executive committee meetings. There can no longer be silos of influence within the organization that the CISO cannot access. When the security of the entire business and of its entire revenue stream is at stake, and a cash injection is needed to boost or enhance cyber security measures, you need to be prepared to make that budget available.

Chapter 9

Lessons Learned — Alarming Trends

A S WE HAVE SEEN IN THIS PART TWO, CISOS STILL SEEM to be challenged with getting a seat at the executive table despite the number of global breaches occurring across organizations — and C-suite's obvious responsibility for cybersecurity.

Compounding this absence at the table are scenarios where a company has placed the cybersecurity program in the hands of a CIO or CTO — neither of whom may be engaged in security activities or as well versed in them as a CISO. In addition to cybersecurity not being part of their education or job functions, the main tasks of IT leaders can often conflict with cybersecurity responsibilities — operational uptime versus minimizing risks, putting systems in production quickly to meet deadlines versus ensuring systems are secure, and there are many others.

It doesn't have to be that way. An organization that has a CISO entrenched in its operations and who speaks both the cyber and business languages of risk and efficiency, will understand that a

CISO can also be a business enabler when the CISO is inter-twined within the business, part of the executive team, has the optimal team structure, and is provided the resources to get the job done. That CISO will understand the business's strategy, the core direction of the company and subsequent initiatives, then plan well to enable the business to move a speed that is aligned with acceptable risks.

We've also come to realize that as business executives, it is important to acknowledge that protecting data and utilizing cybersecurity best practices are everyone's responsibility. All stake-holders in the organization are on point to set the tone; it is true that if you lead, they will follow.

The data, whether financial, personal, or operational data, is growing exponentially. We have come to call it Big Data. But make no mistake — criminals want your data no matter how big or small your organization is; the monetization of that data is what they are after. As we saw previously, the Dark Web is a marketplace for all types of data in addition to arms, drugs, and other nefarious products criminals are known to buy and sell.

Breaches continue to grow in size, be it in lost records or fallout costs. As data continues to multiply throughout society in general, those breaches are only going to get more devastating and create more havoc to your business and/or to the individuals who have trusted you with their data.

Data protection laws that are now starting to be enforced can have significant impact on your business's income statement. Nine figure and multi-million dollar fines are being levied against organizations failing to protect consumer (or employee and third party, for that matter) data. Businesses are being shuttered when they fail to utilize cybersecurity best practices at both ends of the spectrum of protection and recovery.

Not only is there an impact to the organization, key executive leaders are also coming under fire and feeling the impact of mistakes or the lack of a serious approach to what is at stake. Business leaders are unceremoniously terminated as a result of a breach (and not just CISOs), ruining a lifelong career in more cases than you care to know. Cybersecurity should be viewed as an organizational risk and not just an IT or Security risk.

Interactions between the CISO and other executives in meetings should involve a myriad of topics. Based on the size of your organization and its risk tolerance level, here are some topics and questions that can have the greatest impact on the executive leadership team in their efforts to understand cyber-risks and how effective their current cyber program is.

- Have you identified all of your assets (hardware, software, mobile, cloud, data)?

    - Is that inventory maintained in real-time?

    - If not, how often is it updated?

- What is the likelihood, impact, and projected cost of a breach at each of the levels identified?

- Do you have a means to monitor your assets 24/7 for security characteristics and anomalous behaviors that may indicate a potential breach?

- What do you estimate your breach-to-breach response time, aka dwell time, to be?

- With your current cybersecurity strategy and security defenses, how quickly would an attack propagate from perimeter devices to your core infrastructure?

- Where does your greatest cybersecurity risk lie?

  □ How are these risks being mitigated?

- What is your process and the initiatives taken or underway for becoming more cyber-resilient and improving your cyber-maturity rating?

  □ How often is this measured?

- Have you established an enterprise-wide cybersecurity and cyber-risk framework?

  □ Is it adequately budgeted, staffed, and monitored?

- How are you measuring your cybersecurity risks, implementing appropriate controls, and monitoring new technologies upon implementation to ensure your residual risks exposure is at the tolerable level?

- Have you established a process or processes to accept cyber-risk, to remediate those risks, or to fully transfer the risks?

  □ How do these processes affect your financial exposure to those risks?

- Do you have a program in place to gain access to unclassified and/or classified data that can be actioned?

  □ Who is that shared with internally?

- From an organizational perspective, are you able to react appropriately to mitigate and recover from a large-scale breach attempt?

  □ Have you performed this type of exercise to ensure you are cyber-resilient to such scenarios?

- If you had an $X or X% increase in budget, how would you apply that to improving the cybersecurity program?

  □ What other recommendations would you make?

I very much doubt (with all due respect to their expertise) that a CSO, a CIO or a CTO could answer most/any of those questions. You need a CISO!

These questions along with others can open the dialog between the executive team and your CISO. Regardless of whether or not you like the answers, as an executive in your organization it is your job to listen to your CISO or cybersecurity leader's thoughts, work with him on understanding the cyber-risks the organization faces, and proactively drive the organization to provide the CISO and cybersecurity team the resources to mitigate cyber threats to ensure your organization is as cyber resilient as feasibly possible. Accepting the status quo or minimizing what's at stake will only lead to your demise and the demise of many others.

Target Corporation

"I never worry about action, but only inaction."

—WINSTON CHURCHILL

"Inaction breeds doubt and fear. Action breeds confidence and courage. If you want to conquer fear, do not sit home and think about. Go out and get busy."

—DALE CARNEGIE

The Target Corp. Breach — Executives Ousted

LIKE MANY OF YOU READING THIS, I TOO WAS AFFECTED by the Target Corporation breach that started in November of 2013 right around Black Friday.

Obviously, no company wants to be breached, but there couldn't have been a worse time of year for America's second largest retailer to be breached. The breach occurred during the period of November 27, 2013-December 15, 2013. This is the peak of the United States Christmas and holiday shopping season.

Many companies do up to 85% of their electronics, novelty, gift and toy sales during this time of year. To "miss a season" would be financially devastating to most such businesses.

When the dust settled, this breach was discovered to have affected approximately 110 million customers. Initially there were 40 million customers affected by the theft of credit and debit card information. In January 2014, Target stated that a new group of 70 million customers had their personal information compromised that included names, addresses, and phone numbers; there was overlap between the two data sets (card data and PII — personally identifiable information). The total amount of data stolen amounted to roughly 11 gigabytes.

At the time, this breach captured the cybersecurity community's attention and all America's. For the cybersecurity community, it was about the TTPs (Tactics, Techniques, and Procedures) that the attackers used. The initial compromise was of a third-party, an HVAC vendor named Fazio Mechanical, through a phishing campaign using malware named Citadel. Citadel, a spawn of the Zeus banking trojan, was first seen in 2011. Citadel is a very evasive form of malware that at the time could evade many security detection tools and hide in an idle fashion. While in hiding, with its keylogging capabilities, it could then compromise password and authentication systems.

I'll get into the weeds a bit here, but there is importance in knowing the path the attackers took. Once the threat actors had compromised the HVAC vendors credentials, they used them to connect to one of Target's applications that was for vendor use in billing and other vendor administration tasks. From that system, the threat actor exploited the vendor web application to allow them to execute code on the application's server. With a foothold on the application server, the attackers looked for ways to pivot to other points in Target's infrastructure; it performed reconnaissance on the infrastructure.

The attackers found an access token of a Domain Administrator in the compromised application server memory. Domain Admins have god rights in a Microsoft ecosystem. They then created a new Domain Admin account and began to pivot to other systems they previously identified mentioned above. They were able to find the 70 million artifacts of PII (personally identifiable information) from a PCI compliant database using a SQL protocol from a previous pivot point — computer system. They then compromised the PoS (Point-of-Sale) system which is the machine where you insert or swipe your card at the checkout line. With Kaptoxa malware installed on the PoS system, they were able to capture the 40 million credit card information. The final steps were sending this captured information to an FTP (file transfer protocol) computing system within Target's own infrastructure. Then it sent the data to a threat actor-controlled FTP server hosted by a Russian-based hosting service.[1]

I realize this is a lot to take in if you are not familiar with these terms or how threat actors move about infrastructures. But I imagine you are asking, "Where were the security systems?" You may also be asking "Would EMV chips, the little chip on our credit card prevent this?" The use of EMV chips, developed by Europay, Mastercard, and Visa in 1994 would not have helped in the Target case, due to the threat actors using a RAM (Random Access Memory) scrapper on the PoS (Point of Sale) system and, of course, wouldn't have prevented the PII compromise from the database server.

During this breach, there were indicators that something

---

1   For a graphic of the Anatomy of the Target Retailer Breach, visit
https://securityintelligence.com/target-breach-protect-against-similar-attacks-retailers/

was amiss during the breach. Target had installed a new security system by FireEye, which was detecting unusual activity. The alerts persisted, but Target chose inaction because the system was new. They also had deactivated part of the system that could have helped prevent the attack from being successful — done, again, because it was new, and they were unfamiliar with the system. I speculate that it was still being tuned.

An anti-virus system Target had deployed detected malicious activity. More inaction. McAfee, a global cybersecurity firm, manager of Threat Intelligence Service stated, "As an attack, it is extremely unimpressive and unremarkable." Indeed, one can hardly state that — given the alarms the incident created and the fact the threat actor exfiltrated the data out unencrypted. Sounds impressive and remarkable to me (as I'm sure it did to the cyberhacker team that achieved it!) ...

It is hard to comprehend why many alarms were ignored or why the system was not tuned to automatically delete the malware or the very least quarantine it. Perhaps (and many speculate) that Target was receiving so many alerts that they got overlooked. Maybe they didn't have the right incident response process that escalated the events to the right levels. A Target spokesperson stated the team did investigate but what they found did not warrant immediate follow-up.

Obviously, there are many lessons to be learned. The main lesson is about follow up on alerts, but here are more:

- Escalating alerts to appropriate levels and taking action to determine a root cause.

- Installing sophisticated malware across all systems may have caught the HVAC compromise.

- Insisting on vendors using two-factor authentication when connecting to systems.

- Requiring Domain Admins to use two-factor authentication for any activity.

- Alerting appropriate personnel when a Domain Admin account is created.

- Having sophisticated monitoring systems could have alerted on a number of the techniques.

- Blocking external data transfer to Russia or any other country; at the least if communication to the country is needed, only allow activity from and to a specific IP address.

In the end, this incident was very costly and not just to customers. Target lost millions upon millions of dollars (some estimated nearly $1B) due to the breach. Net earnings were down by over a billion dollars from FY 2012 to 2013; Q4 earnings were down 46% from 2012 to 2013, Q1 earnings were down 16% from 2013 to 2014, and Q2 earnings were down 62% from 2013 to 2014. Over 140 lawsuits were filed against Target with shareholders being part of the lawsuits filed. Target's stock price took a hit as well.

A little over a year after the breach, in March 2013, Target's CIO (Chief Information Officer) resigned. Target's President and CEO resigned in May 2014; he was a 30-year veteran of the company, but Target struggled in vain to gain back customer trust. Oh, and what happened to their CISO (Chief Information Security

Officer)? NOTHING! Why not, you must be asking — after all, wouldn't he have been the front-line executive whose head they put on the chopping block. Yes, he would. But... they did not have a CISO at the time...

PART THREE

The Board
of Directors

A S A MEMBER OF ANY BUSINESS'S BOARD, YOU ARE called on to provide oversight to this company. As a seasoned and thus older business professional, cyber security for you might still be "that guy in the basement" or the IT team that's holed up in the server room. That might well have been the case when you started out in management 30+ years ago, but times have been changing!

In a 2015 McKinsey survey called *Cracking the Digital Code: McKinsey Global Survey Results*, only 17% of directors said their boards were sponsoring digital use and protection projects. That was just 5 short years ago — in a time we were already seeing alarming cyber breaches with their data theft and malicious manipulations. Only 16% of directors said they fully understood how moving into the digital age would disrupt their industry, their own business and consumer expectations of the business.

If cybercriminals are not waiting for you to figure out how to commit breaches against your businesses, you cannot wait any longer, either. They are not waiting for you to get informed, get proactive, or start thinking strategically about the future of cyber space and your business.

Today, to stay relevant and to rise into the expectations of defending the business's relevance and strategic growth for this business, you need to be "digitally literate" and continuously engaged in the protection of the company. You need knowledge about cyber threats and the type of Cyber Security Program the business requires. Knowledge and curiosity about this aspect of the business will allow you to provide educated oversight.

Chapter 10

Why You Are Needed Now More Than Ever

2OTH CENTURY BOARDS DIDN'T HAVE TO BOTHER WITH cyber risks, because for most of the century they didn't exist! Today things have dramatically changed, as you know.

You are an officer of the company and the 21st century's cyber risks will henceforth require your oversight and regular attention. Cyber risk assessment and cyber protection are now part of your mandate. Your personal and professional reputation and future are at risk should you fail. From now on, it is vital for your personal and professional reputation, the reputation of the Board, C-suite, and the business as a whole that you keep your eye on the Cyber Ball. Reading this entire book is a good first start but be prepared for continuous education and involvement. Today, it just comes with the BoD's territory.

McKinsey and countless other surveyors make it clear: Cyber Security and a keen understanding of cyber risks is our #1 concern. Boards of Directors must move beyond their traditional roles and move into proactive thinking and execution around Cyber Security/Cyber Risks.

Close the Literacy 101 Gap

As a Director, you need to understand the cyber risks to this company in your care. At a national level, the US has long understood the need (review *Senate Bill S.536 — Cybersecurity Disclosure Act of 2017*. It states that you have an obligation "to promote transparency in the oversight of cybersecurity risks at publicly traded companies.")

You personally need cyber literacy whether your business is listed or not — in order to know the potential damage the company might suffer. Intensive reading helps. Questioning the CISO as your board's go-to educator is essential. Remaining curious and thinking about future potential threats and preventing them is the board member's new job.

You must not only get assurances that the CEO is on top of such risks on a daily basis, but also that a well-educated and experienced individual has been hired as CISO for the business and welcomed into the executive hierarchy as a full and vital member of the executive arm of the business.

Once the CISO is chosen/hired, require that the CISO give the board periodic reports. That means you will acquire the foundational education/cyber literacy to understand 1) what the CISO is saying to you and 2) the right questions to ask of the CISO about the business's cyber risks and protections.

You need to be assured that the company has a Cyber Program which includes enterprise-wide cyber awareness training. Your cyber literacy allows you to understand the Program's nature and purposes, and that it is functioning as well as or better than your peers' programs. By "peers" I mean a layer of organizations — those other companies for which you are a Director, all competitors (direct and indirect) in this industry, other similarly regulated/at risk businesses.

Make sure that there is someone on the Board (and it is ideally all of you) who speaks the language of Cyber Security and can/will ask the hard questions. This Cyber or Digital Director must understand all the answers you are given and be an interface to the Board to make the various circumstances and security needs clear.

Cyber Literacy 201

More boards fail to cyber-defend their business due to the questions they hesitate to ask, refuse, or simply fail to ask than for the questions they will ask.

Rule of Thumb: Never hesitate to state bluntly to the CISO, "We don't know what we don't know. What are the questions we need to ask you? What information are you dying to give us that we have either been shoving aside or not realized was essential?" The CISO gets it: You don't have the background, education and training he/she does in cyber. The CISO gives it to you as needed.

Cyber Literacy 201 requires that you recognize when you are nitpicking over details and not seeing or blatantly ignoring the big picture crisis. This might work for a politician's spin doctors, but not you.

Likewise, just because you are faced with and trying to manage the fallout from one attention-grabbing breach, don't fail to broaden your view and ask the CISO what other risks are present right now alongside the current breach that need resources, tools, budget, attention.

Cyber Risk Is Data Risk

The business you are in (and today that is all businesses in all industries and sectors) has massive amounts of data — it collects information hourly, stores it, manipulates it analytically to improve the various types of operations it engages in, uses the information for reporting and legal filings of all kinds.

Today small, medium, and large to gigantic businesses across our economies have a cyber-intoxicating range of assets. While I'd like you to note that mid-market businesses are the ones most at risk, all of us are data-rich and will eventually be targets. These data assets start from the top and trickle down through and out of the organization: infrastructure, software applications, managed and unmanaged endpoints (in-house and mobile), Internet of Things devices and connections, cloud services, etc. There are thousands of passwords to be managed (or hacked). There might be thousands of assets and access points to your data that are not under your control, and thus even more easily hacked than those within your cyber security program control.

Just consider that every internet-connected element can be attacked in myriad ways. The business — whatever the business might be — is rich in cyber-stored data.

There are also cascades of risk. You are at risk by the fact of dealing with third parties. What is their access to your data? Who do they turn around and share that access or data with? Those become your fourth-party risk factors. You have a richer level of risks than you think.

The key word there is "rich". To cyber threat actors, every bit of data you produce represents wealth for them.

Cyber Risk Is People Risk

Cyber threat actors — from nation states to the competing company right across town — have motivations that you must try to comprehend. Yes, it about monetizing your data to their benefit, but the motivations don't stop there. Thus, your risks don't stop there, either.

The first person at risk is the Top Leader. That might be you or the CEO. It is certainly the CISO as your frontline executive in all things cyber. Perhaps the CFO is the target with financial breach types.

Bottom line: If you don't want to make headline news, understanding the business's cyber-talk, cyber risks, cyber program hand-in-hand with the CISO is vital to you (and I mean you personally) not becoming the scapegoat for the breach.

Next are the business's employees at all levels of the business. You have people's livelihood in your hands and that livelihood is what the cyber criminals are after.

They want your company and employee data/information for their profit, to simply disrupt your business momentarily, to harass and stalk individual employees and stakeholders, to put you out of business, to exact revenge (think internal cyber threats by personally disgruntled or ideologically motivated staff or contractors) ...

Your business perhaps manages your employees' 401(k) or pension accounts internally. That is data that is highly coveted by cyber criminals because it is real cash right now to them. They can sell and resell that information many times over ...

Perhaps your business is part of a traded mutual fund or listed on the stock exchange. Cyber criminals disrupt your business to the point of devaluing your business and decimating its value on the exchanges. However brief that devaluation, the business, its reputation and accumulated market and consumer trust evaporates for a much longer period...

Reasons for cyber breaches are various, curious, and always nefarious. Keep brainstorming the potential motivators of the criminal mind, try to think like a hacker, and be very afraid. Afraid enough to take the actions that defend your business.

Should your company be breached or otherwise targeted, you cannot shut the barn door after the horses have stampeded out. Proactivity is the rule. If your business is not protecting itself, there may soon be no business to protect. Forward thinking is why you are needed by the company. As a board member, you must be part of the protective solutions keeping the cyber threats at bay and keep cyber actors looking elsewhere for their payday.

Protecting your business is a daily obligation. It is critical and from here on out, it is your job.

You waste the loss you have in the case of past breaches if you don't learn from the catastrophe. Learning about cybersecurity must not be just intellectual. People's livelihoods and security, their safety and the very existence of your business are at stake.

> *"You waste the loss[es] if you don't incorporate them into how you do business in the future."* —Chris Hadfield, *Fighter pilot, astronaut, Commander of the ISS (International Space Station)*

Hadfield wasn't talking about cyber but about the lives of astronauts in those rocket launches that went wrong. But you get the point. Your board — the second kind of board — is involved in the excitement of the business, in understanding the risks inherent in the business model, and motivated to solve the problems.

Chapter 11

So That's What a CISO Looks Like

THE BOARD OF DIRECTORS NEEDS TO ENGAGE DIRECTLY and often with the Chief Information Security Officer of the company. This may include hiring a new CISO at some point, so you'll need to understand the skills, education, and experience — and personality — to look for in a great CISO.

The first consideration is your business's needs moving into a future of increasing cyber threats. If it already employs a CIO and/or a CTO, you must consider the protective value of adding a CISO and charging him/her with cyber program responsibilities, as this professional is focused on cyber threats, threat actors within and outside the business and measures that can be taken to minimize and eliminate risks.

Today's cyber threats have long been knocking at the door of businesses of all industries and all sizes, regulated industries, and others. Thus, you need layers of protection that levels of trained teams can provide. Your former IT department may have been divided (or urgently need to be) into a number of different teams each with distinct operational/security functions and operating respectively under the CIO, the CTO and the CISO. In many organizations, the CIO oversees it all. This may be a mistake if operational priorities are amplified well ahead of cyber threats and a solid Cyber Defense Program or if you've not provided the right structure and resources for your CISO to succeed.

Depending again on the size and structure of your business, the CISO might report to a CIO who in turn reports to the board and CEO. If this is the case for your business, do not mistake the CISO for a purely technical manager! A CISO is, by training and function, a long-term strategist and as such is able to view current threats in light of future impact and then to reduce or eliminate those future risks with actions taken today. Strategic cybersecurity is a core function of the company and enables all parts of its operations to function safely on a daily basis, with little to no visible interference and no interruption to business continuity.

Thus, the larger or more regulated your business, the nearer to the board the CISO should (must!) be and the more frequently he should (must!) be consulted and heard. At a minimum, he should be on the organizational chart with a strong dotted line to both the CEO and the Board. This said, in highly regulated industries (e.g., banking, pharmaceutical, healthcare, nuclear) required to respect stiff compliance requirements, your CISO might report directly to the CEO, or to the COO, CFO, the General Counsel, or the CRO (Chief Risk Officer).

For the continuity of secure business operations, you must not restrict the access of your CISO to all other executives and directors, nor underestimate his influence on the future strategic cyber protections your business needs. Again, the CISO really must be placed on the top line of C-suite executives on your org chart and involved in all aspects of the business and strategic discussions as an equal executive partner. I come back to this need again and again: The CISO is a full executive member of C-suite and must be heard as all other executives are. He must have the respect and the ear of his peers for the reason I will now explain (and which joins all other reasons for him to be trusted).

According to Harvard Business Review's Analytic Services Survey (May 2019), *"The CISO is no longer just another function within IT. The role has expanded to include more of the characteristics of a business leader."*

The survey results showed that "48% say one of the CISO's top 5 responsibilities is to build an organization-wide cyber-security culture; 63% say this will be a top 5 responsibility in three years. 84% of respondents consider the ability to educate and collaborate across the business to be very important in a CISO."

As you interview and prepare to select a CISO, your Board of Directors needs to be aware of a specific C-suite behavior that puts the company at great cyber risk. Because of this risk you must hire a CISO with the personality, "the chops", to manage this particular risk, among others.

The risk is right in the C-suite: With all the perks and influence that come with an executive position, C-Suite executives are often notoriously tempted to throw their weight and influence behind curtailing cyber security defenses affecting them personally. This can occur more often than you think when executives feel tight security protocols unnecessarily control them (they who are so trusted!) and should not apply to them.

That is why when the CISO says, "NO!" to opening up cyber protections "just for them", his fellow executives must be willing to listen and unquestioningly accept the advice!

In a MobileIron study called *Trouble at the Top*:

- 47% of executives surveyed had asked for access to unsupported devices

- 45% asked to bypass multi-factor authentication processes

- 37% asked for access to business data on an unauthorized app or device

- One-third used the same password for multiple resources

- 62% thought that additional security measures made their devices less usable

- 68% of executives surveyed were concerned about their personal privacy thinking low-level IT staff had full access to their data and devices

- 58% were intimidated by the complexity of IT security

In total, 78% of those surveyed had asked to bypass one or more security measures. In many organizations, C-suite have the highest level of access to company data and systems. If their email accounts or security credentials are compromised (i.e.: stolen by hackers through the lowered security measures the executive has demanded and obtained), threat actors now have access to the entire treasury of business information you possess.

Do not let your C-suite be the door through which risks enter your business. Cyber security is not the cops! Cyber security, the team and its measures are fully mature partners in the business you operate. The CISO needs to stand firm before his peers and deny them any breach-creating privileges — and he must not be fired just because he is doing this particular protective job! Don't let executives be the portal to your data and business operations that can later be held hostage by threat actors! Make sure your CIO, CTO, CISO (and lower level IT personnel whom executives might feel they can "influence" more quickly) are likewise prohibited from waiving any security measures — whoever has requested or demanded them. That includes you.

Other Considerations of a CISO

The CISO is your educator in all thing's cyber security related. But you must not be a passive learner. In order to evaluate and contribute to the company's protection, you as board member will need to possess a foundational awareness of the cyber risks to your business (additional to C-suite itself as a risk). Get educated yourself in the various forms cyber fraud can take on and their prevention methods. Get a good grasp of the wide-ranging types of cyber threats your business may be victim to. Understand your business's types of cyber-exposure, but also how peers' experiences (competing businesses in this industry and other-industry businesses you are also a Director for) can inform your protective measures in this business. Understand how federal and local regulations your business must respect are connected to your presence in cyberspace and create risk.

When you have such a foundation, communicating with your CISO will come more easily to you. However, don't stop there: Have the CISO educate you every single time you interact. Get him involved in budgeting discussions. Have industry regulatory discussions with him. You are both up to the minute in projected and enacted legislative bills so as to project the business's current and future needs related to compliance to them. Have the CISO explain why various new tools are periodically needed and justified in the budget.

Speak the Language

The board and the other C-suite executives need to agree on hiring a CISO who is "bilingual", but not in the usual sense. This executive must speak that deeply technical "Geek" language, no doubt about it. But not with you! That is why the CISO must also speak "Boardroom", understand business risks. Those two "languages" are necessary for him to be effective as a leader for two groups of collaborators: Those on his cybersecurity team (while he also stays educated on the deeply technical side of cyber security evolution); those C-suite executives and directors whom he must apprise of the status and new needs of the company's security in terms everyone can understand.

Your CISO will not need to be so deep in his technical practice that he works with the FBI, but could he qualify to do so? Knowing your CISO is a specialist that can speak on that level, knowledgeable and well enough known by that level of authority to represent you should be a comfort (and perhaps a job requirement). It requires big picture business thinking with deep-rooted technical knowledge.

Spend, Save or Profit?

This is another key to the highest cybersecurity performance your business can achieve: Stop looking at cybersecurity as a cost center. Also refrain from looking at cyber security programs as purely savings mechanism: While cyber security measures cost money, they pay for themselves by prevention of costly breaches (whose remedies may be unaffordable, such as in ransom cases). Instead, look at cyber security and the cyber security teams you employ as core to the business. Look at cyber security as a way to preserve the profits you are making.

Profile of a CISO

Technically, CISOs are deep in the weeds of the cyber security and possess a wide range of understanding of subjects such as cyber security and risk frameworks; technologies past and presents; fraud and anti-money laundering schemes; cyber related regulations applying to your industry; in-house (staff) and external partner (contractor, vendor) access controls. They are continuously on the lookout for new cyber threats, threat actors and "holes" in your systems. Your best choice for a CISO is connected with professional cyber security professional organizations. He might possess multi-industry experience or be a long-time professional in your own industry (and this will be one of your strategic choices to make). He is an individual that may have an advanced degree and possess many certifications. He may serve on industry related Boards as well; not afraid to network and be peers with law enforcement and government agencies. These characteristics show that he is a lifelong learner and up to the responsibility of a CISO. Beyond this, what is the profile of the best CISO?

Q: How important are each of the following skills to being a successful CISO/cybersecurity leader?

% of respondents who say this skill is very important

Skill	%
Ability to educate and collaborate across the business	84%
Ability to communicate (oral and written)	82%
Ability to take data-driven decisions and smart risks	79%
Strategic insight/ability	79%
Leadership skills	76%
Ability to recognize and nurture innovation	73%
Team-building skills	68%
Executive presence	65%
Ability to mentor talent	62%

Source: Harvard Business Review Analytic Services Survey, May 2019

https://www.pwc.com/us/en/services/consulting/cybersecurity/
pwc-final-hbr-pulse-pwc-5.pdf

The CISO for your business is:

- an executive with clearly defined lines of responsibility in relation to a CIO and CTO and to the rest of C-suite

- a mature executive presence

- armed with 15+ years of experience and strong Cyber Security Program leadership history

- the one security leader with enterprise-wide responsibility, engaging daily with all the functions and layers within your company

- may carry multiple certifications such as, a Certified Information Systems Security Professional (CISSP), a Certified Information Security Manager (CISM), a Certified in Risk and Information Systems Control (CRISC), and/or others in the security and IT disciplines

- adept at listening, data gathering and synthesizing of information

- expert at explaining, training and persuading people at all levels, in the language they understand, about data/information security and the types of risks directly connected to the jobs they perform

- an excellent people and thing manager

- both strategic and tactical

- clear on security, risk and compliance issues for this specific industry

- active (hands-on) in monitoring, repelling, and responding to cyberthreats

- an immediate (i.e. today's threat level and responses), short-term (i.e. quarterly/annual) and long-term (i.e. three-five-year) security planner

- skilled at and empowered to make business-based risk management decisions

- the company's cyber risk educator and influencer

- skilled at benchmarking/metrics so as to measure Cyber Security Program effectiveness and communicate it to non-technical partners

- continuously educating self, team, partners because "90% of the world's data has been generated in just the past 2 years"

- able to craft valuable reports for tech and non-tech readers (C-suite, board, other stakeholders, managers and — often overlooked — rank and file staff)

This latter ability is important for a real reason: Three quarters of business leaders estimate that employee negligence and lack of awareness is a top cyber risk. CISOs agree! Thus, the CISO has to be an authoritative, persuasive educator at all levels of the organization. Your department heads must make this education mandatory, and free up team time for it on a recurring basis.

As you consider your current or future CISO (and although this takes additional interview time to assess), does this CISO have the mature, cool and calm personality to evaluate and defend the business against a growing and perhaps staggering volume of cyber threats?

And lastly as to this professional's background, consider what professional roles this individual has performed in the past, and where.

Your CISO will definitely need to be that technical professional with whom you and your non-technical board members can communicate. This is because you will be asking for reports from the CISO including: cyber risks the business is facing; what mitigating or eliminating steps are being taken; how cyber incidents are/have been handled and what is being done to mitigate them; how your cyber/information security program is doing (you might have various projects underway, and get statistics and metrics on them); how budgets/requested funds are being spent.

Chapter 12

Your CISO — CTO, CIO, or IT Exec, Team

ARE THE LEADERS AND TEAM MEMBERS OF YOUR CYBER security program up to the cybersecurity game? It is true that, historically, cyber security was ensured by the IT team and that was that. This is a brand new (digitized, internet-facing) world...

You may remember I mentioned a National Defense company that discovered their CTO was not up to the cyber security game, much to their chagrin. I hope you understand at this point of your reading that a CIO/CTO and a CISO have different training and experience and perform functions that are complementary to each other rather than a substitute for one another. A notable difference (and potential conflict) is that a CIO/CTO's main job is to ensure technology is functioning — and it is sometimes made to happen at the expense of data and system security.

Though I have brought up these points elsewhere in these pages, a cyber security program and a CISO with the authority and resources to succeed is not a reality in all organizations, even major billion-dollar corporations. Yet an experienced CISO with the right team (in number and in skillsets) is crucial to your business security. Through poor appreciation for the executive role a CISO performs, a C-Suite or board of directors may shackle not only the executive himself but the very cyber security the CISO has been charged to defend.

Cyber security is ensured across a large ecosystem comprised of all your company's departments and operations and calls on the cooperation and buy-in of all your executives and directors. Cyber security is not performed in a silo.

The first thing to check is this: Are other members of the C-team and the entire board of directors in agreement on the need for a CISO in the first place? The CISO will not be effective and is a waste of good money if that is not the case.

If yes, are all of you willing to make the CISO a fully-fledged member of the executive team? This means the CISO will participate in all executive meetings and be granted consultative access to all other C-Suite executives as regards cyber security. By now, you should not be wondering why this is necessary. By now you should understand that cybercriminals access your organization from every tiny little opening in the cyber security wall they can find or create themselves due to your inattention. They do not care if it's through your customer service system. They do not care if it's through your marketing department employees. They do not care if it's in the warehouse that they gain access to your data. All they are after is access.

As stated, the board will be expected to gain sufficient knowledge of cybersecurity so that when they put the CISO and his presentations on the agenda at least four times a year, at least one board member can understand the implications of the review and any new resources/changes the CISO is requesting. Granting the chief information security officer a few minutes per meeting won't cut it; cyber security is multilayered and multifaceted, and you need to understand your organization's state of security, know the nature of past breaches and fixes, know who your cyber enemies are and your company's security needs moving forward. If that takes a longer time than you had planned, make it happen anyway.

85% of consumers will not do business with a company if they have doubts about its security and privacy practices. This was revealed in the PwC report, September 2017. Don't be one of those organizations!

Once you have determined that the CISO is "one of you", and again depending on the size of your organization, who this executive reports directly to, should be a logical chain of command. Keep in mind that if you also employ a CTO and CIO, the CISO will not report to either of them in order to avoid conflicts of functional interest. Instead consider that the CISO would more logically report to the CFO, your Chief Risk Officer, or the CEO. That is the way to avoid "functional conflicts of interest" amongst CIO, CTO and CISO.

The second thing to consider while evaluating whether your cyber security teams are up to the task, is whether you have budgeted, and your CISO has recruited, a full cyber security team to protect your organization. Face the fact that the larger your organization, the larger your cyber security team will need to be (just as in most other functions you hire for). A survey of 250 companies in different industries showed that how big your cyber security team should depend on a number of factors. If you have a hefty dollar budget or whether you have attracted a seasoned CISO will be factors. Many businesses state that a general rule is that cyber security staff runs approximately 10% of total IT staff. Another rule seen is to hire cyber security team members (engineer/analyst/cyber-specialist attorney and so on) per 1000 employees, depending the industry and data at risk this multiplier can fluctuate greatly: 4 or 5 for high risk industries. Your C-suite and the board should analyze this together.

Also understand that recruiting and hiring such specialist staff will not come cheap. These are not entry level positions. They are all 6-figure salaries and rest assured — they not only earn but are worth every penny. Keep disaster scenarios in mind before starting to complain about the cyber payroll: Locked out of your own business through ransomware and revenues down to nothing until the incident is settled? What is *that* cost? Additionally, their respective continuing professional education must be part of the budget. This should come as no surprise as you know now that cybercriminals are always creating and inventing new ways to hack you.

Your third major consideration when evaluating your cyber security teams and especially your CISO is the amount of autonomy your organization gives to this executive. I've discussed this, but if any executive on your C-Suite needs to be able to make instant decisions and turn on a dime, it will be your CISO. This means he must not have a chain of command through which is funneled his problem and proposed solution set. He must be able to act on his own to the degree needed, not wait for a committee to come to a decision days or weeks too late.

The CISO community, like many other professions, is a tight-knit group of people with at least one thing in common; we all want to do good. By nature, we are people that want to help. We want to preserve and care for what we have been charged with. As CISOs, we "mine" the collective knowledge base and insights that our fellow CISOs and friends possess; there is great strength in numbers. Rely on this body of professionals as a company through your own CISO.

Go Virtual Here, Too

Depending on the size of your company and given that such professionals command 6-figure base pay salaries (and depending on where you are in the country, your industry, the size of your company that can be from $150,000 to $500,000 annually or more), you may need to start out with a solution other than hiring a full-time CISO. That other solution is to hire a v-CISO, a virtual CISO; businesses even consider supplementing their CISO or using a v-CISO for projects. Today, it is a fairly common solution for businesses unable to afford a full-time salaried CISO, but who already recognized that having the expertise on tap is critical to ongoing operations.

Don't shy away from such a solution. Your business has undoubtedly hired remote workers and a wide range of specialist or technical contractors in the past (contract or gig workers). Many successful and swiftly growing businesses have "kicked it up a notch" so to speak by hiring virtual management or executive support, such as a shared human resource director or an on-demand (virtual) chief financial officer. This gives the business some financial wiggle room — but also the expertise — until full-time salaries for such experts become affordable.

The only difference here is the highly specialized, technical, strategic, analytical skill set that the v-CISO brings to the business. Indeed, a virtual CISO brings your company his high-level experience, education, analytical skills and deep familiarity with cyber security threat actors and cyber security programs. A virtual chief information security officer will interact with your company, your departments, and your people on demand, typically at fees around 35 to 45% of a full-time salary depending on the hours you require their services.

As well as being on demand, the v-CISO might provide expertise on specific cyber projects your executive team has already identified, such as bringing the company into HIPAA or other compliance or providing a cyber risk analysis of your current or proposed new vendors. The virtual CISO may help you craft in-house digital policies and procedures or help C-suite understand and set the standards that needed across the organization for a more robust cyber security.

As a matter of law, keep in mind that cyber security legislation (most of it is at a state level at this writing) is recent, but officials are paying attention. The New York State Department of Financial Services (NYDFS) Cybersecurity Regulation actually requires that companies employ a CISO. It will not be long at all until California, Illinois, Texas, and other big corporate HQ centers across the land imitate New York, with the remaining states following suit like dominoes.

What Needs Protecting?

Your leadership will come to a point where you need to determine how much you have to protect. What are your data assets? If those assets were compromised, would your business be shut down? Seriously impeded? Massively devalued?

Consider that your data assets are like bankable cash, and also consider how frequently mergers and acquisitions occur in our economy. You do not want your data assets to be at risk when this will reduce the overall cash value of your entire business. Like Marriott's breach which involved theft of 500 million customer records (with customers fleeing the hotel group for a more cyber secure competitor), or like Yahoo's valuation nose dive after a massive breach of its core data assets (buyer Verizon discounted its original buy price by nearly 25%, and later settled for about 15% less than the starting offer), you don't want to lose customers or business value at any time — much less during a multi-billion dollar M&A!

Another consideration when thinking about hiring a virtual or salaried CISO is how complex your organization has become since its inception. Businesses that grow organically sometimes build a complex web of layers upon the original business foundation, and some of the coherency and security gets lost in the growth.

If you are part of a regulated industry, cyber protection is a must-have. But if you and your cofounders, executives, board members are by choice or by nature quite conservative or simply have a low risk tolerance, cyber security measures are also a given. You need a chief information security officer, whether virtual or on salary, along with the range of specialist team members the CISO requests.

Chapter 13

A Cyber Security Program Explained

EXPLAINING WHAT A CYBER SECURITY PROGRAM IS CAN be quite simple — in spite of the reality that the complexities and multifaceted nature of cybersecurity tactics and defensive measures are mind-boggling for the nontechnical individual.

In a nutshell, a formal, budgeted Cyber Security Program protects your Internet-connected hardware, software and the data your business creates, collects and uses on a daily operational basis; it protects data stored on/accessed from your own proprietary servers or in the cloud.

Further, the Program considers and defends against the more expected and common threats that businesses of all sizes and types suffer (viruses, phishing) to the headlining-making breaches and business-devastating threats such as ransomware attacks locking your systems or holding your data hostage, or theft of millions of customers' private identification data in your care.

Lastly, a Cyber Security Program includes both human resources (your highly trained cyber security personnel) and the tools they use.

Incident Response Plan

Such a program also includes a tested, trained Incident Response Plan which involves not only CISO's team but others across the business. Such a plan detects incidents such as internal breaches, external attacks, or attack attempts, unauthorized (intentional, accidental) data sharing or attempts at data access, losses or thefts of physical devices. Once detected, the plan presents the processes and procedures the response team will take. Is the Incident Response Plan robust enough for your business's needs as well as tried and tested? Is it clear who leads the response team (CISO, CIO, external forensic partners etc.)?

In case of a breach — and you know this if you have read media reports of competitors or other-industry breaches that have made headlines — other members of your business will need to be involved in the incident response process. These others inside your business that you will immediately call upon for non-technical "breach management" support may include your media communications or public relations manager (downplaying the dramatic media representations of the breach while it is dealt with internally) as well as your General Counsel or legal affairs department personnel (notifying customers and anyone else potentially affected by the breach). Depending on your internal budget and the design of your cyber security program, it will be internal executives or managers working independently on remediation. It might be the CISO working in collaboration with previously retained external partners who manage such aspects as forensic investigation (to fully understand the source and nature of the breach).

C-suite and boards overwhelmingly agree that a robust Cyber Security Program includes five areas of capability: identification, prevention, detection, response, and remediation. It will include *identification* of assets within you infrastructure; *application* security which are measures embedded in your software applications to prevent hacking; *information* security which prevents unauthorized use of your data; *network* security, including both software and hardware protection measures; a disaster *recovery* and *business continuity* plan; *operational* security measures; a user *education* plan.

The question is: What level of Cyber Security Program is in place right now in your business?

Inventory Your Data Assets

Without getting too deep into the weeds of such Programs (as I promised you), you start where you are, and do an inventory. Creating a robust Cyber Security Program starts with an inventory of your data assets. It needs to be a real time, up-to-the-minute inventory of internet-facing and internet-connected assets as well as those that are not now connected but might potentially be at any future time. You must include the entire spectrum of your business assets; no type of data or information or access tool is "exempt". Think about all hardware (including mobile devices), unmanaged assets, cloud services and IoT applications. You cannot protect what you do not know exists within your infrastructure.

Documented inventory is first, followed by how your teams are able to continuously monitor all the security aspects of those assets. These include asset discovery, classification of assets by criticality, risks associated with specific asset types, third-party management, and strong governance around each. The governance can be through a well-known framework such as NIST, ISO or other hybrid approach.

Protecting the Crown Jewels and Detecting Threats

What are the ways you can qualify and quantify the strength of your cyber defenses applied to each of those assets? This considers your capabilities to limit the number of and impact of breaches. This involves the appropriate safeguards your program needs to put in place to ensure delivery of critical services and services in general through your asset portfolio.

Continuous monitoring and detection processes as well as a response plan are all vital parts of your Cyber Security Program. Ask your CISO about the sophistication and measurable effectiveness of security systems that have been implemented; about the protection of all user accounts including the administrator account (often a weak link). Ask about the ability to detect a cybersecurity event quickly which allows you to mitigate the breach-to-breach response gap (where the risks are) to as minimal amount of time as acceptable.

Areas related to this part of your Program would include identity and access management, tools related to data security such as data loss prevention, cloud access security brokers, endpoint protection, cloud security protection, etc.

Code Red! Respond and Recover

If there is an area of your program you don't want to shortcut, it is in how your organization responds to an incident. Paraphrasing

Allen Iverson, the Philadelphia 76'ers great, "I mean we're talking about practice!" For cyber security, "response" means that you and all appropriate staff PRACTICE, PRACTICE, PRACTICE!

Responding swiftly and appropriately to any incident can be the difference between a breach event with no damage done by the threat actor, and a breach event that allows the threat actor to exfiltrate your entire customer database or card transactions or your detailed bid on Gulf Coast oil reserves before you even know you have been hit.

Going through the security process again, a complete inventory of assets is first. You then can protect what you have identified. If you have not fully protected some asset, threat actors get through. Detection of that breach is next. You see the urgency of detection skill and timeliness, because by definition detection must precede any response. Once detected, your response protocol kicks in. Only then can you analyze the nature/source of the breach and improve your defenses.

Though a breach is bad, preventing the threat actor from exfiltrating any data allows you to claim a small victory and go back to the protection and detection drawing board.

With excellent responses, recovery is more about lessons learned and process improvement rather than just "Oh, we did not respond well, therefore we have to restore our entire server infrastructure from backups". The latter does not close the gaps through which the hackers entered your business.

A strong response/recovery plan, a strong backup strategy, and an ability to execute the business recovery and business continuity plans seamlessly can make all the difference. In the case of your failure, it results in a business going out of business. In the case of success, it means the business is still alive and well and continuing to serve customers and clients.

Maturity Is a Constant Evolution

An important aspect of any Information Security/Cybersecurity Program is the ability to measure the effectiveness, examine where you are at a particular point in time, make the appropriate adjustments for your desired state (make improvements), then re-measure. This is known as a maturity model.

There are many maturity models available from the DoD (US Department of Defense), NIST (the US National Institute of Standards and Technology), ISO (The International Organization for Standardization), CIS (The Center for Internet Security®), COBIT (Control Objectives for Information and Related Technologies), or the FFIEC (The Federal Financial Institutions Examination Council).

Models consist of various maturity processes and levels, cybersecurity requirements and best practices, and controls required to meet each level of the model. Most are robust in nature and can provide your organization a great roadmap to follow to its desired state. As a general approach:

- The CIS model would be ideal for smaller organization or those wanting a quick snapshot of where they are at.

- The ISO model is more often used for non-US organizations.

- The FFIEC and its Cybersecurity Assessment Tool (CAT) is primarily for financial organizations, but the maturity section can be used by all organizations.

- The NIST model is probably the most often used.

High Level NIST Framework Diagram

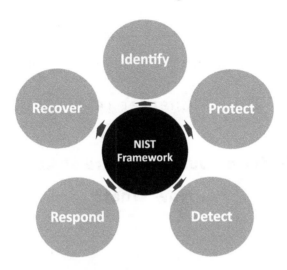

NIST Cybersecurity Framework Detail

NIST Dimension	Definition	Examples	
Identify — What assets should we protect?	Enterprise understanding of what assets and data exist and should be protected	Asset Mgmt. Bus. Environment Governance	Strategy Risk Mgmt. Third Party
Protect — How should we be protecting assets?	Appropriate Safeguards to ensure delivery of critical services	Identity Mgmt. Access Control Data Security	Information Protect Maintenance Protective Tech.
Detect — How do we detect threats?	Appropriate activities to identify the occurrence of a cybersecurity event	Anomalies and Events Detection Processes	Security Continuous Monitoring
Respond — How are we responding to threats?	Appropriate activities to perform regarding a detected cybersecurity incident	Response Planning Communications	Analysis, Mitigation, and Improvements
Recover — How do we recover from incidents?	Appropriate activities to maintain plans for resilience and restore due to an incident	Recovery Planning Process Improvements	Communications

Chapter 14

The CISO Has Our (the Board's) Attention — Now What?

"60 percent of organizations have their CISO at key board meetings, but only half of business executives think the role has a high level of influence on management decisions."

FROM CAPGEMINI'S *THE MODERN, CONNECTED CISO* REPORT

I WRITE THIS CHAPTER NOT ONLY FOR THE BOARD OF DI-rectors who are reading but hopefully for a CISO reader as well. I've already stated my view that a CISO must be heard at every board meeting and consulted by the board's cyber specialist outside those meetings as need arises. It is time to move the arrow up from 60% attendance of CISOs at board meetings to 100% presence.

As a CISO myself, I obviously have a few thoughts about the relationship between a CISO and the Board — what that interaction should be at best to protect the business and keep all parties apprised of risks and remedies. Perhaps your CISO should read this, too, so that everyone is on the same page. In all cases:

- I implore directors to assist the CISO in every way possible to communicate his messages to you.

- I implore CISOs to make every effort to be clear and understood by these non-technical partners you have in the Boardroom.

As we all very likely realize, we technical people need lots more training, practice and attention to our presentation and communication skills since we are the ones who need to be "bi-lingual" and able to speak convincingly to both technical teams and non-technical teams. If you are a CEO or a board member reading this, don't just cringe at your technical officer's presentation skills but make sure he signs up and follows high-quality training to improve those skills. The health and continuity of your business depends on the CISO being able to communicate vital information to non-technical people, so I invite you to help him in all the ways you can.

I will state once again that a CISO should be a top-line executive on your organizational chart and, if that is not how you see things, the CISO still must have *at a minimum* solid line or dotted line connections on the organizational chart to the CEO, with periodic access to the board during their scheduled meetings.

A CISO has best success when he remembers that a Board of Directors (and most all of the business's other stakeholders) is 95-100% non-technical people. A CISO has success when he can adjust his language to help them understand, and at a level of detail that is appropriate. This is where I again say a CISO has to be "bilingual" to meet all his obligations — he needs to "speak Geek" to his technical team members and his supply chain of vendors and contractors; he needs to pivot and "speak Boardroom" when addressing non-technical executives and directors and outside stakeholders. A CISO will be asking the same questions to his team in geek-speak as he must answer to the other executives and directors in boardroom-speak. This takes awareness, and for some CISOs (no offense meant), serious training and regular practice!

I beg other non-technical stakeholders to bear with a new CISO until your languages intersect and you understand each other; speak with your CISO and let him know what you value most in a board presentation and in presenting to you. Non-technical stakeholders will need to hold their ground when asking for clarifications from the CISO and in turn the CISO will pare away the technical aspects to bring the risks and remedies into a purely business level of explanations.

It Is about Governance

A CISO is a key factor in assisting all of C-suite, directors, and other stakeholders in their governance capacity. After all, if governance is "the system by which an organization is controlled and operates, and the mechanisms by which it and its people are held to account" — then knowing the cyber security status of any of today's businesses is a vital piece of this obligation.

It is also vital for business risk management and business continuity for the directors to know their cyber security team, their past experience and current roles — before any operations-threatening breach occurs. This logically starts with getting to know your CISO.

The basic information stakeholders need to have: A run-down or real and potential risks to the business; protections that can and must be put in place and continuously upgraded and monitored; costs and tools needed to implement the security measures that make the business and its people safe.

Best Practices from the Board's Side of the Table

Know your cyber security team *before* your business is slapped with a $230M fine such as British Airways was (the EU's response to the 2018 data breach of British Airways that exposed the sensitive data of around 500,000 customers). If you do any level of business in European Union nations, be aware that the EU's General Data Protection Regulation or GDPR has teeth!

Know your CISO team's protective measures before you experience a breach like the one closer to home of Capital One — over 100 million US and Canadian clients' data was stolen (the hacker also skipped away with 140,000 US Social Security numbers; 1M Canadian Social Insurance numbers; linked bank account numbers for over 80,000 of the company's credit card clients ...).

Can your business come back after either type of massive breach? Making sure it can and does is the "raison d'être" of your Cyber Security Program.

Directors must realize that cyber threats are not a matter of if but a question of when. To date, almost every major business has been breached; those in charge who deny they've ever been breached have likely just not discovered it yet... Formulate all of your questions to the CISO with this in mind. Grant justified and reasonable budget amounts to the cyber security team in view to pushing back all types and levels of potential future risks — not just the ways and means to remedy past ones.

There are three steps to take at the board level to prepare to interact with your chief information security officer. I have touched on these somewhat but again, they are:

First, make sure your board has at minimum one cybersecurity knowledgeable director who participates in all meetings when the CISO presents. If you don't, add one. This director can beneficially be hands-on outside board meetings by going into the business and familiarizing himself with operations, hot points for cyber threats and the protective measures in place; visits might be coordinated by the appropriate C-suite executives and department heads. This is a role that a v-CISO (Virtual CISO) could fill as well as be a sounding board for the incumbent CISO or individual in the CISO role.

Second, if your Board of Directors has formed specific subcommittees, make sure one of them is accountable for cyber security as a (new) priority. Very often in larger businesses this is the audit subcommittee taking this on but may also be the responsibility of the risk subcommittee or a specifically formed cyber security subcommittee.

Third, ask the hard or clumsy questions in whatever words you have. The CISO gets it: You are not a technically trained person and his job is, in part, to give you the confidence of understanding a complex topic. Together you can clarify what information you seek and the CISO will formulate and reformulate his answers until you have understanding. This is tough but be prepared for bad news as well as good news: Cyber space is evolving every minute of every day and keeping your security program up-to-the-minute is a challenge at every level of its implementation. Crap happens and will happen less often if you face down your security needs in strategically in concert with the CISO's recommendations.

Some high-level cyber security questions non-technical

stakeholders want to ask and that need regular review and new answers by the CISO for the board's information and consideration are:

- How safe are we as a business on a scale of 0-5?

- How much will the repair and install/testing of new protections after the breach concerning _____ cost us?

- How much time will that take to implement?

- What new training for staff is needed — and what benefit to the business does that training provide?

More business-centric questions all directors must ask include naturally:

- How much does continuous and/or enhanced safety cost us?

- What is the defensive purpose of your requested new purchase/installation of _____?

- What resources will it save us?

- What new resources will it call for?

Best Practices from the CISO's Side of Things

This is some reflection on how a CISO should interact with his board. CISOs — please read this!

The CISO job is almost a "Renaissance Man" position since the role (with the cyber security teams) is to protect and prevent, monitor, and detect, recover, and remedy, manage and educate about risk. The role also means the CISO is bilingual as discussed and can turn on a dime to apply a new strategy to a new type of threat or threat actor. It is indeed a multi-faceted role.

So, I arrive at six best practices for a CISO when working with a Board of Directors:

First, get your presentation skills for non-technical audiences up to professional grade! We CISOs rank dead last among all C-Suite executives in our presentation skills, so make that learning effort. This should include non-technical writing skills and public speaking/presenting skills (including what makes it to your PowerPoint slides), because — while the board's job is to manage risk including cyber risk to the business — they are just not all technical people.

Second, and somewhat related to the first point, is that you need to keep in mind that board members understand "business" risks but are not as well versed in "technical" risks to the business. The CISO must learn to summarize in writing all the technical details, somewhat simplify complex topics (without dumbing them down) and state clearly what the current business-critical risks are. While drafting such written reports or presentation handouts, always remember that this is for non-technical stakeholder consumption.

Third, get in the habit of preparing written pre-meeting reading materials to inform board members in their own time about the current status of high-profile security risks (including actual breaches the company has suffered and the effectiveness of measures taken) and other pertinent contextual information they need before your personal presentation to them. Contextual (or "put them in the picture") information can include education such as global cyber threat and cyber security program trends; security strategy insights; security spending in your own industry as versus others; etc.

Fourth, in a short-timed live presentation, the CISO must give the directors a funneled context of the cyber security topics he will be addressing. This is not usually a repeat of the pre-reading report, unless the board has pointed questions. Start with a general or big picture executive summary — sort of a "telling them what you will be telling them" overview. This might include updates to your business's threat landscape (new threats on the horizon/past breaches dealt with) or the status of upgrades to your cyber security program. Create visuals such as charts and dashboards that are still at the top (general) part of your funnel. A dashboard may indicate number of new threats identified and whether remedied/not remedied; the number of failed threats/ breaches; how many additional compliance standards have been met; etc. Work down the funnel with more details you believe the board will require for any decision making. Some of those details might include how the failed breach might have affected the business if it had succeeded.

Fifth, be prepared to enumerate the types of threat actors that are potentially targeting the business and give a brief profile of each one and their supposed motivations. If they are nation states (and they will be attacking more types of industries than uninformed board members might think), say so. If they are internal actors, never ever hesitate to say so. But the CISO has to be prepared as well to enumerate the preventions being put in place to block such threats and threat actors.

Lastly, be prepared to:

1) bring one new educational item to the board per live presentation.

For instance, answer the questions, "What is malware? What risks do we have from such a threat? What defenses have we put in place to block them?"

2) answer "quantitative" questions succinctly.

Such questions are about KPIs — what the metrics are that assure you that improvements are real, that performance is being tracked, the metrics that show a decline in protections and what to do about it; but be careful not to use too many metrics that is foreign or not meaningful to the board. The board is cognizant of competition and will also be asking you, the CISO, how this business of yours compares in preparedness and protections to competing companies.

Chapter 15

The Governance of Cyber — Find It or They'll Find You

C YBER SECURITY IS AN ENTERPRISE-WIDE RISK MANAGE-
ment issue — there is no backing away anytime soon from
this reality.

I briefly mentioned governance in the last chapter. It is the
purview of the Board of Directors, with cyber security matters
now an integral part of that governance. Cyber security has long
since left the job description of the IT team and is now in the
hands of the CISO and his team, alongside the entire C-suite
and board.

The cyber threats and the cyber adversaries you are facing and
what the company needs from the board has decidedly evolved.
There are some basic principles for board level cyber security
oversight that have been tried and tested in public and private
sectors. There are legal, market, financial and broad-based operational considerations in the governance of an enterprise and all

of those circle back to your business's cyber security program and its myriad defenses. There are expectations you can set for your CEO and C-Suite about cyber security programs and reporting.

Start with Cyber Literacy

How to govern a company when it comes to cyber space risks and threats and the choices involved in a cyber security program?

As a baseline in your governance of cyber, the company might need you to free up a budget to improve the Cyber Security Program. It might need your support to facilitate the rollout of an improved cyber security program or other high level, resource-intensive measures.

Just as the CISO is at best a "bilingual" member of C-suite, every member of the board must possess a basic degree of cyber literacy as well. Again, moving into our digital, internet-facing futures, there is no getting around this requirement. In order to know the right questions to ask or reporting to require, board members must know what the business's most valuable assets are, how its digital systems interact with those assets, and to what degree those assets can be fully protected. Which of the assets are core to business continuity?

What threat actors or types of breach does possession of these assets open you up to? Face the music and realize that insider threats are also very real and put defenses in place for those as well. Engage the C-suite so they do not short circuit security measures at their own whim. I discussed this very real cyber risk earlier. Do not ignore the need for all-staff digital security training and regular refresher courses — that is where you are the partner to HR and ask to know the training program that has been devised and administered; better yet help develop it with them.

In other words, everyone up and down the hierarchy needs to acquire cyber literacy and understand cyber defenses and their role in deploying them.

Once you know that basic amount of information, you can question the CISO about the risk level of your core most valuable assets and the resources needed to protect them and work outwards to protections of other assets from there. You get information about the cyber security program your CISO, CIO and CTO agree you need, and compare it to the ones in place at peer organizations. Is your program robust enough or over the top (where "over the top" does not refer to cost alone)? Learn what a NIST Cybersecurity Framework is and should look like for your enterprise.

Constant Change Is the Only Constant

Now that you have the high-level picture of the business's digital-facing assets and the potential cyber threats to them, you must stay apprised. The CISO and C-suite executives must apprise you of all breaches and their degree of severity — and request an analysis of how it happened and new preventative measures taken. Differently stated, the Board of Directors must have a process through which it is systematically informed of breaches, severity/impact, remedies. Don't be cut out of the loop or fooled by an executive dismissively saying, "Oh, we took care of that." Ask and get clear answers to the question, "If a cyber threat actor wanted to cut us to our knees, how would he go about it? How do we protect against this worst-case scenario threat?"

Also, under the board of directors' purview must be added all the new cybersecurity considerations when there are major shifts in the business model. To remain relevant, seize market opportunities, to gain efficiencies, to deepen profits — you might be led to make changes in your business model, its markets, its management approaches. They also open the business up, at the time of each such change, to new cyber threats.

Such shifts might include mergers and acquisitions, brand new partnerships, or joint ventures with other firms (third party cyber risks). It might be from brand new product launches and entering new international markets. It might be from hardware upgrades or replacements that risk enters the picture. Today, in our Internet connected world, every shift opens your business to new cyber risks and your CISO must be involved right alongside the executive managing that shift.

Don't let your departments create silos where information is not shared. While these might not be considered insider threats, they can become so. In other words, with the best intentions, department heads and executives make changes and do not re-member the intricacies of cyber security when they do so — and create a hole through which hackers and all types of threat actors can enter the business. In our world, there is no more place for "secret" or undisclosed internal changes. The risks to the entire business are too great.

Your CISO and his team is your business's defense backstop in the case of any change the business undertakes or shift that is imposed upon it.

Take to heart the need to involve the CISO in all kinds of business change. Never think, "Oh, the CISO is in no way con-cerned with this matter." No silos! As an example, your legal department and your CISO will need to collaborate in many different kinds of situations to maintain a high level of cyber defenses. For instance, if a merger is masterminded by finance and legal, never count out the CISO who can bring a risk assessment connected to this merger to the table. New partners call for new assessments and very likely for new protections. New partners mean that those partner organizations need to be as cybersecure as your own — or more so. Find out. There will be new costs or other resources involved in protecting your business before, during and after that merger.

Your business might likewise be regulated, but don't let legal run alone in tracking new cybersecurity related legislation or new industry regulations. New regulations call for new digital operations which in turn call for new cyber protections and additional budgets.

The same warning applies to other department heads and C-suite executives when they mastermind other types of shifts in the business's direction or daily operations. For instance, the CMO might quite naturally involve the CFO as they jointly work on strategies to open new foreign markets, or to fund and launch new product lines promoted in perhaps new ways. The CISO needs to be a partner in the process as well, to understand the desired strategy, assess how the company opens itself to new risks when the strategy is implemented, to build in new appropriate protections.

Look at the CISO as a change *facilitator*.

Another type of change hit us all between the eyes in the first quarter of 2020 with COVID-19. Many businesses defaulted immediately to remote work and work-from-home scenarios — with all the breach and misuse risks that has already involved. Is your national defense corporation equipped to ensure top security in this new scenario, knowing that VPN access to your data by staff is not the only defense you need (and knowing that vishing and phishing have allowed hackers to gain entry into your VPN as well?)? A CISO needs to be involved, assess, put in place defenses/

protocols that are 100% obeyed by all staff. Many businesses are playing catch-up. Cyber threat actors have not been waiting around for you to patch things up tight!

Again, though it seems unwieldy, you need to look upon your CISO as a change facilitator!

The key governance message here is that you don't react, but instead act proactively, strategically, with "cyber literacy" and with deep respect for the fast-evolving nature of cyber threats to your organization.

Chapter 16

What Boards Are Doing Today

IN OUR CYBER-RISKY WORLD, THINGS ARE FINALLY CHANG-
ing at the board room level. But frankly, there are still two kinds
of Boards of Directors as regards cyber security. Stakeholders of
any enterprise need to make sure it is governed by the second
kind rather than the first. The costs of having the wrong kind of
Board of Directors in place are far too high in terms of money,
reputation, and business (dis)continuity.

The First Kind

The first kind of board is failing in its efforts, or worse. "Worse"
means you have been an obstacle to a cyber secure enterprise.

This Board of Directors is blatantly ignoring the need to evaluate and protect the business against cyber threats as "not our job as
directors". They are ignoring the evolution of governance in light
of all businesses' presence in cyber space, the creativity of threat

actors to interfere with the most basic of business operations all the way to inserting themselves in the most subtle, destructive and costly ways. They refuse to add cyber risk to the risk assessments they perform, monitor, and move to remedy.

These boards are the ones unwilling to step up and learn more about the cyber world, the cyber risks of the business they govern and the threat actors pounding down the cyber doors (or sneaking through them). They don't see a cyber security program as any part of their governance role (although I hope the preceding chapter has changed your perspective).

Vast numbers of boards are failing; not seeing cyber as their purview because as they state, "IT's got it covered". They are ignoring the CISO and his team which they see as just more "technical geeks". They are hands-off regarding everything digital, internet-facing and data related. They do not expect, much less require, an annual "state of cyber" presentation by any of C-suite or any member of "IT".

These failing boards have no one knowledgeable on the board about cyber, nor do they seek out expertise outside the board or the enterprise.

If this board is not paying attention to cyber today, how can it govern a budget and the overall risk to the business? This board has its head in the sand about the extent to which businesses are internet-connected but also internet-dependent. In its strategic guidance of the business, such boards look at the financial and operational health of the organization while totally ignoring its cyber health … and never acknowledge that its cyber health creates the very foundation for that desired financial and operational state of wellness.

This type of board — the unprepared, unwilling type — will still be victim to our relentless "24-hour news cycle". If you are a director of such a board, and a breach of any media-worthy proportion occurs in your company on your watch, be prepared to see your name in the headlines. And not in a good way…

This "no-cyber corporate governance" model is now obsolete. Without a cyber governance component, the board itself becomes obsolete — soon putting itself out of business.

The Second Kind

The second kind of Board of Directors sees the enterprise's cyber security as one of their definite areas of governance. This board sees that a Cyber Security Program and interaction with the organization's CISO fits squarely in the "box of risks" that they manage. They also see that an optimal Cyber Security Program is a business enabler, distinguishes them from others.

This second kind of board will charge the CISO with the Cyber Security Program and will be providing the resources (structure, tools, budget) the CISO requires to get the job done. In exchange, they put the CISO on their quarterly agenda and pay attention to those frequent, regular updates and reports from this executive. That means this board gives the CISO abundant time on each of their meeting agendas — they get that a few minutes won't do it.

This board is proactive in understanding enterprise-wide risks and tracing the effectiveness of the business's Cyber Security Program, its degree of effectiveness and maturity, and the specific and ongoing general cyber health of the company.

This second type of Board is proactive, informed, forward-thinking and strategic about cyber security. They know that cyber risk is fluid, multifaceted, multi-sourced and ever-evolving — ever-present. But they always feel up to the task!

These directors understand the business's absolute and nearly total dependence on the internet in all its operations across the enterprise. These mature directors willingly admit that governance is a brand-new ballgame when contrasted to the business tools and business risks of their early career — and they are open to learn.

This kind of board recognizes that the impact can either be like that of swatting a mosquito from your ear repeatedly from failed attempts to breach your systems... and go all the way to a sudden, single, devastating, business crippling incident from a threat actor you did not predict was even in the wings. These directors know that they cannot be complacent about security when their CISO tells them about the multiple attempts successfully blocked, because the big business-halting one could be right around the corner.

Good boards have one digital-savvy director (or more) at the table. If they do not or cannot, they have outside expertise of the highest state-of-the-minute quality on tap. These boards are the ones training not only themselves on cyber security, but ensuring that the business is training all staff (up and down the hierarchy from the mailroom to C-suite) and developing cyber security awareness at all levels of the company and with all the types of third party partners it works with.

The board meets with the CISO regularly, reads the material provided by him before the meeting and is keenly aware through media and their professional networks of the cyberattacks competitors and other peer organizations have faced.

This kind of Board of Directors acquires the knowledge and understanding of the risks both great and small, and makes sure the CISO, CIO, CTO and all of C-suite have the resources to implement the best solutions to it.

There is no cyber risk area too obscure for their attention — everything from internet-facing promotional marketing, to supply chain security, to individual client credit card transactions — and no discussion of cyber security program needs are too time-consuming.

This proactive board also understands that they (like the CISO) need to think "other-culturally" because cyber threat actors come from around the world where mindsets are very different about the sanctity of private property (aka your "not-so-propriety-anymore" data). They know they also need to think "other generationally" since notably nation state threat actors are continuously training talented teenagers (sometimes the age of a director's grandchildren) to hack, ransom, steal, vandalize and bang on the cyber doors of your business.

Standards and New Governance Approaches

By paying attention to cyber risks of the past and of the present, you govern better into the future.

Just saying "We have a good IT team" is not a good prevention or security posture and will not create the cyber security standards you will henceforth need. Moving to the cloud, changes in your autonomous systems, changes in your process automation tools, more and more Big Data to manage by multiple authorized user parties all open the enterprise up to new cyber risks. Business-to-business interfaces evolve and the processes of third-party vendors where you trust the other business to have just as robust a cyber security program as you do — or better — also make for new cyber risks to predict and prevent.

Your board might operate through committees. Reconsider the cyber needs of any business and you must conclude that — though the initial risks are assessed, and the initial cyber security program evaluated by a cyber subcommittee — the risks are undeniably enterprise-wide. Because cyber risk is across the business, governance must leave the subcommittee and be a topic of general board discussions at each and every meeting.

In a nutshell: Cybersecurity has become a board-wide responsibility on the best boards. The CISO and the informed experts he brings in must have your ear.

These comments of mine come as US states — New York and California were the first — begin to legislate cyber risk responsibilities. More and more states are faced with consumer protection demands. Never forget that your customers and consumers, third party vendors and all your partners worldwide read the media reports on cyber incidents. States are pushed to create more pieces of legislation, including standards of cyber security within your business and fines to those businesses not up to those standards.

To make sure legislation is relevant while being at the same time robust but not too restricting, boards need to precede the state legislatures rather than take and wait-and-see stance. Boards need to encourage their management to be the standard of excellence that legislators look to and consult as they craft new laws, standards, and fines. Boards need to reach out proactively when it has become clear that states are moving into a regulatory position and offer their experiences and guidance from a governance standpoint.

Equifax Breach

"The greatest leader is not necessarily the one who does the greatest things. He is the one that gets the people to do the greatest things."

—RONALD REAGAN

"Leadership is lifting a person's vision to high sights, the raising of a person's performance to a higher standard, the building of a personality beyond its normal limitations."

—PETER F. DRUCKER

Equifax and Board Responsibility

IF YOU HAVE READ THIS BOOK IN ITS DESIGNED SEQUENCE or even just this section, you probably understand a Board of Director's enormous responsibility for and impact on a company's cybersecurity program. Though a Board of Directors may not have the deep cybersecurity knowledge of those on a cybersecurity team, they should at a minimum be trained on cybersecurity risks and be able to ask the right questions to the leadership team and the CISO.

In Board study after study, cybersecurity risk is one of the top concerns of Boards across the globe. Boards everywhere should be knowledgeable about the damages a major cybersecurity breach can cause to a company and its shareholders. A Board of Directors needs to be aware of how governance ineffectiveness can directly impact the members of the Board.

The Yahoo settlement in 2019 changed the dynamics on how Boards are held accountable. It was the first-time former officers and directors agreed to pay a settlement for breaching their duties in a cyber-related incident.

I am sure many of you reading this were personally affected by the Equifax breach. As I stated elsewhere, and as most consumers know, Equifax is in one business — the data business. If any enterprise should be protecting data assets, it is the business whose sole reason for existence is … data!

More than likely if you have ever had your credit pulled, you were affected; PII (personally identifiable information) for over 147 million United States, UK, and Canadian consumers was compromised; most were United States consumers. Data stolen included Social Security numbers, driver's license numbers, names, birth dates, and addresses. And like so many other breaches, there were warning signs and a number of security mishaps that could have prevented or lessened the impact.

Unfortunately, a major breach can happen due to a single exposed resource. Cybersecurity teams have to get it right 100% of the time; a threat actor has to be right just once out of hundreds or thousands of attempts. This is the dilemma many cybersecurity and IT teams face today.

In the case of Equifax, the breach started due to a consumer complaint web portal being unpatched. The missing patch was to mitigate an extensively known vulnerability, CVE-2017-5638, in Apache Struts which are used for creating Java web applications. The patch was released on March 7, 2017. I am guessing that web portal received a lot more traffic after the breach became public.

Interestingly enough, the Department of Homeland Security warned Equifax of the vulnerability. They did not apply the patch at that time, but instead waited for over four months until July 29, 2017 to do something about it. Why July 29, 2017? Equifax noticed anomalous activity on their network. The threat actors access the systems between mid-May and July 2017.

Let me stress this, so that it is abundantly clear to you: If the Department of Homeland Security takes the time to make a phone call to your organization telling you to patch a system, you better damn well do it by the end of the day! This includes the work-interrupting step of fully rebooting the system and then validating the patch you applied.

Be that as it may. There were a few missteps in this incident. One, they had hired cybersecurity firm Mandiant to perform an assessment due to other recent incidents where criminals accessed their systems via information, they had been able to acquire from other non-Equifax incidents. Mandiant warned Equifax about unpatched systems as well as misconfigured systems. Equifax did not have sufficient segmentation and had left usernames and passwords exposed in plain text. Equifax failed to renew an encryption certificate which contributed to the threat actors exfiltrating the data in encrypted form. The incident reaction was also criticized due to it not being made public until a month after Equifax discovered it. Further making themselves targets of public criticism, company executives sold stock around this time. Talk about insider information!

The breach caused reactions by local, state, and national government agencies, from lawsuits to new laws to congressional hearings to reforms on breach notification and consumer control over their credit reports. Numerous investigations ensued, including one on (you guessed it) insider trading. The CEO Richard Smith resigned.

In 2017, Equifax settled lawsuits that include up to $425 million to help consumers affected by the breach. Though members of the Board of Directors were reelected by shareholders in 2018 (the first election after the breach), many investment firms and entities campaigned to not re-elect members; votes against Board members tallied above 30% and 35% for a couple of members.

The United States Department of Justice charged four Chinese military-hackers in connection to the Equifax breach. An investigative team made up of a multi-national coalition traced the digital steps to identify the threat actors behind the breach. During the announcement, The United States Department of Justice noted other breaches (Office of Personnel Management, Marriott, and Anthem) that they believed the Chinese government was behind.

With new regulations and breach investigations determining Boards to have lacked oversight, there is no shortage of headwinds Boards will face. In short, litigation related to cybersecurity incidents has increased where plaintiffs allege individual Board members to have breached their fiduciary duties. Do you need any further encouragement to become a hands-on cyber-educated, security-involved member of the Board?

I am reminded of a quote by John D. Rockefeller, *"Don't be afraid to give up the good to go for the great."* Boards of Directors: The ball is in your court to go forth and be not just good, but great.

PART FOUR

YOU
and the Small
Business Owner

I HAVE HEARD MANY HORROR STORIES ABOUT HIGHLY educated, business-savvy individuals who protect their companies' data like their very lives depended on it from 9-5, only to go home to be a virtual open door to hackers and cyber threat actors through their personal electronics, applications, home-use IoT technologies, personal email and financial accounts — and devil-may-care usage of them.

From home security cameras with a default setting to broadcast everything they film on the Internet (a real and fairly recent Chinese product sold on both eBay and Amazon, and the broadcasting done as a factory default setting no one pays attention to examining, much less changing) to letting your young children play with your high security clearance business smartphone, I have seen otherwise intelligent individuals do some silly things in their homes that leave them wide open to cyber threat actors.

If you realized the extent to which you are personally letting yourself be tracked, monitored, connected to, viewed, heard, recorded, and traced, you would get very nervous indeed. Yet we are heedless.

I know influential executives whose business email account is protected by two level authentication access, but whose door to their $1,000,000 homes is protected by a $10 digital lock that they have programmed to open with their four digit birthdate (and whose entire extended family and "close" friends know this…). Their personal email account password is their oldest child's birthdate.

Really? What is wrong with that picture? Take everything you are learning in these pages home with you. Take all your new cyber security knowledge into your home, teach it to your family, and protect your property. Protect your belongings. But above all protect yourself and your family members.

Digital stalking is real. The Dark Web sells spyware that should rightly be called stalking-ware because that is how the dark websites selling it are promoting it to buyers. You might certainly want to know where your children are, but do you want all of the Dark Web to know, too?

Take just as robust a set of precautions with the myriad internet-facing devices and apps you use in the home as you do in your business. Your family's well-being may depend on the cyber security measures you put in place.

Chapter 17

Security at Home — Your Family and Kids' Future Depend on It

THE DIGITAL FOOTPRINT THAT YOU LEAVE BEHIND IS ALL about data. Personally identifying data. Data that can track you to within inches of where you are standing.

While you leave your footprints in the digital transactions you perform at work, you cannot forget the footprints you leave when you use digital devices and do any Internet-facing transactions for your personal affairs and in your homes.

When your elders or your minor children use such devices and perform such transactions, they are at a special risk of cyberattacks, because threat actors view them as particularly naive and vulnerable — and will go after them sooner rather than later. You must protect them, though they protest loudly. They are in your care.

These more personal transactions you must shield can include everything from using an app uploaded to your personal smartphone (online banking app, food delivery app, fitness app, online calendar...) to entering a password (into your online stock trading page), to opening, reading and responding to a personal email appearing to be from your bank (but in fact a phishing attempt to collect your personal identifying information), or using any of the social media platforms found online today (Twitter, Facebook, Pinterest...). When you get in your computer-run, internet-facing car, remember you are in a hackable vehicle...

Think hard about the profile of the threat actors we discussed a few chapters back. Do you really want them shoulder-to-shoulder with your elementary school aged (grand)child?

When you have a business-issued smartphone, such as National Defense companies issue to their personnel with top security clearances, realize that your employer does not always prevent you from uploading a smartphone app of your choice. They might detect it days or weeks later and ask you to remove it, but you are probably able to load it. Many a father and grandfather have allowed children and grandchildren to upload "game" apps to their supposedly secure and reserved-for-business-only phone only to discover that the game app is owned by and a conduit to Chinese hackers or Russian hackers (this happened to a well-known National Defense company's entire set of newly-issued smartphones as recently as July 2020, with two game apps detected on numerous company smartphones). Do those hackers know that this is your business phone? Why take the risk? Keep it out of everyone else's hands. Protect it with passwords and perhaps thumbprint authentication (your CISO might require you to do so anyway). And don't give it to anyone else, no matter how much you love them...

Well, I do not want to get too deep into the weeds (as promised) of personal protections that you can take for yourself and your family members. Just take a moment to think about 1) the internet facing devices and apps you have in the home and 2) all the little scams your various family members might fall prey to. Identify (and shut down tightly) the hacker-friendly openings you yourself innocently create for the hacker:

- That phishing email telling you that there are "changes to your credit report and click here to see them"...and you clicked.

- Not immediately dealing with that unsettling social media follower's messages to your minor (grand)daughter. And she's feeling harassed, tracked, and scared to death.

- Your own elder mother getting a phone call from "her trading account manager" and asking her to create new passwords or to confirm her identity — *over the phone* — by giving the caller her social security number. Sit and have a cybersecurity talk with mom.

- Getting a voicemail from the Social Security Administration asking you to create an online account (and the caller says he'll walk you through it — all he needs is your name, address, SSN...!). The government and its various agencies never, ever phone us. Just hang up.

- Not using a spam filter on your email account. Even web-based accounts such as Yahoo! have robust spam filters, so use them. Even if it means checking through the list of spam messages before each major deletion of them.

- Keeping all your passwords on an Excel worksheet stored with no password access on your home laptop desktop. Password vaults or managers are free (two of the top on the market today are Dashlane and LastPass). The investment of time to set one of them up is worth it for peace of mind.

- Not using the password managers' 'password generation' tools — systematically. We all "default" too easily into memorable passwords and you don't want any of those!

- Again, having easily remembered passwords because you are not using a password vault or a password generation tool. Let me repeat: Those tools can create complex, highly secure passwords for you and remember them for you.

- Not investing in a home-network firewall or ant-virus software for your various home-use devices.

- Never backing up your home data. Use a robust external drive to do so rather than USB sticks.

- Not upgrading or updating software applications on your home equipment. Hackers know all the ways into those older programs! Upgrade them.

- Not understanding social engineering and the cyber risks that presents to your family.

Protect Yourself; Protect Your Children

Social media threat actors and risks to your kids are real, so do not treat them as just a passing irritation. Online bullying is one level of harassment and intrusion. Deal with that as you deal with other intrusions that can happen over social media, Instant Messaging, phone.

The more often our children carry around smartphones (and they do), and the younger they start doing so (and it is far too young an age for them to imagine all the risks), the higher their cyber risk. But that internet-facing smartphone is not the only source of your children's personal data, nor is their school laptop.

Beware the School System

Kids' data resides in school databases (elementary through graduate schools; private and public schools). Have no doubt: Criminals steal it.

Case in point: The school system of a prosperous valley town near Los Angeles saw one of its elementary school system's database and network ransomed in mid-September 2020. Why an elementary school?

Walk through the logic of it based on the knowledge you have from reading this book until this chapter. Put yourself into the cybercriminal profile. What does a cybercriminal want? Data that he can resell! If he can hack into a prosperous community's elementary school system, he can discover who those "rich and prosperous" parents are, where they live, what their phone numbers and email addresses are. That is a rich haul indeed for a cyber hacker! And... cybercriminal bonus... They know where the children are and can threaten their physical/cyber safety to get what they want from the parents.

Years later there might be ramifications when the child enters the adult world. The older child holds (or tries to qualify for) his first credit card; it is only at that time that all the past illicit use of his identify becomes known, since those transactions will now appear on his personal credit report! All sorts of false usage of identity can ruin their start in the world of adults.

Schools are wide open to data theft and criminal use of it simply because they typically do not have the cybersecurity programs in place that large or even medium sized corporations can afford and implement.

Remember this and take measures: Identify theft is not limited to adults.

Criminals can easily find out where you and your minor children are almost all the time. School data, social media postings and email blasts about school events of all types, (and even those "no-tech" vehicle bumper stickers that boast your children is an Honor Student at X School) tell criminals where to find you — and them.

Social Engineering

I've mentioned social engineering a couple of times in passing. Understanding what social engineering is, and the many forms it can take will help you protect your family against such malicious activities.

Indeed, social engineering uses many hacking approaches to get you and your family members to give up certain information that is valuable to the hacker. It is called "social", because it is founded on human relationships (as developed notably on social media platforms) and human feelings (curiosity, pride, fear). In short, hackers use a range of psychological tricks and traps to draw you in to giving them the information they want.

Social engineers are hackers. Have no doubt. If an email you received is disturbing or alarming in any way, delete it before opening and never, ever take the action it wants you to take.

If there is a too good to be true offer on a website that you are scanning, believe that you will get into trouble if you follow through on it. You might see some of this in social media advertising, where is a blast and add to millions of eyeballs in hopes that just a few dozen (who knows, maybe a few thousands) will respond.

Among other social engineering tactics there are scareware, pretexting, fishing, and spear phishing.

Scareware uses fear and threats, false alarms, and make-believe threats to lead you to believe that your system is infected and that you need to install their protective software immediately. What they don't tell you is that their protective software is that malware.! When you get pop-up messages on any web screen saying "your computer might be infected with spyware (malware) so click here for a protective tool" — don't do it.

Pretexting is a lie. The hacker starts by creating some trust with the victim and to do so might impersonate coworkers, your bank's officials, an agent of your tax office or some other sort of authority. From that basis of trust, they ask you for personal data and ways to confirm your identification. They'll ask for Social Security numbers, personal address and even perhaps bank account numbers or bank records, or security information about your business or employer company.

Lest you not be frightened enough yet to do a major overhaul of your home devices and installation, remember the Dark Web?

That is where child pornography and spyware can be bought and sold. That is where your various (easy) passwords are being sold and resold so that criminals can cash in before you button things up. Protect your minor children. Protect all members of your family.

But the Dark Web is not by far the only place where your personal data can be hacked. Where is the feed from your security cameras going? Are you sure you have only the cameras that you wanted and only in the rooms you chose?

When you think cyber security, remember the ways you live your life outside the business. Protect yourself. Protect your money, your possessions, your identity. And your loved ones. Your company CISO does not help you at home... but maybe the Board in collaboration with C-suite should put together a Cyber Safety at Home training seminar for all staff...

Measures to Take Now

If protection has become your mindset, then you know the next thing: Practice safe cybersecurity hygiene.

Protect your data with the various simple techniques available to you. As an individual (or as a school student or employee anywhere for that matter), you should protect all of your passwords with personal "password vault" such as Dashlane or LastPass. And need I state that ...

1) your passwords must be unique or one-use-only; no more using the same password on every site for every login! Cybercriminals love when you "go the easy route". Don't.

2) your passwords should be very complex in nature. Make them of great length (12+ characters), use upper and lowercase letters, numbers, symbols. Have the password vault create the password for you and let it remember it when you need to log in. Even better is to use two-factor authentication when available — a password and a token that is sent to your mobile phone for example.

Another protection measure is concerning your finances. Monitor your credit report constantly and set alerts for every time your report changes (for better or for worse); question why it got better and what happened to "ding" your score downward. Go a step further and lock your credit file to prevent threat actors or anyone with access to your personal data from obtaining credit in your name without you knowing. This is also a good practice if you have children or grandchildren under the age of 18.

If you can, you should use a credit card instead of a debit card when making purchases anywhere (online and in person). This is for your protection and it is good discipline. The damage from using a credit card exclusively is that your credit card is maxed out. The advantage is that if there are malicious/suspicious charges you can dispute them and fairly easily get a new card issued to you. If it is your debit card, it can be disputed, but it takes more time to resolve and you may need the cash in the bank during that period. It also helps develop good financial practices in budgeting to pay off the credit card every month. My caution to you is if you practice this, please pay off the credit card every month.

Whether at home, at your own business or at work as an employee at a corporation, backing up or storing your data to a safe location is also a critical practice you should utilize. Most home users do not back up critical data; buy an external hard drive and copy files to it periodically. Keep it separate from your computer.

There are many other critical cybersecurity practices to learn about that can raise your cyber hygiene level. These might include...

- not using outdated operating systems (in other words, invest in a new PC and in the up-to-date versions of your commonly used software applications);

- changing baseline security settings (on your email account and on your internet search engine) to better harden the system;

- changing factory default passwords that come with new Wi-Fi routers to something more complex;

- keeping important financial or healthcare account numbers readily available but safe;

- not retaining data that you no longer need;

- and my all-time cringe-worthy favorite: not plastering the internet (social media sites) with your personal data.

I have heard my fair share of social media horror stories and any single one of them should warn you against posting anything remotely compromising on those sites.

Case in point: A woman won the lottery jackpot and *posted the amount of her multi-million-dollar gain on her social media.*

Not only that, she *named the bank at which she had deposited the funds. The city she lived in was also no secret from prior posts.*

That amount of information is a hacker's dream come true! The point here is to take control of the data that is important to you, your loved ones, your business — to your safety from criminals and to your reputation with those who matter to you. Define more narrowly for yourself and your family what you mean by "personal" and "high risk" and take precautions.

Chapter 18

You Are More Than an Individual Contributor

W E'VE SEEN SOME THINGS TO REMEDY IN YOUR HOME
and for you and your family's cyber security. I hope you
are frightened enough of the potential risks to do them now!

Let's go back, though, to the workplace, and talk about steps
you can take as a "rank and file" non-manager, non-C-suite employee to make your own cyber life and that of your business safer.

Please understand that you definitely do not need to be an
executive or part of the in-house technology team to take charge
of your own job-related cyber security. In fact, when you do take
extra care of your own direct usage and apply all the best defensive
practices, you are going a long way to protect the business that
employs you, too.

*NOTE: If you are an executive, manager, director reading
this, use this section as a guide to educating and training
your team members in "Best Cyber Security Practices". Let
everyone know, and frequently, that each employee up and*

down the hierarchy and in all your locations (today that includes remote workers whether salaried or contractual) is responsible for cyber security whatever the job and whatever the level of data access he/she has been granted.

As such, Directors of the Board and C-suite executives and all managers need to know what Cyber Security Best Practices are and implement best practices across the business as front line users yourselves — or how can you expect buy-in and compliance from staff and management? It is an all-hands responsibility and your responsibility is not only to lead the way by example, but to communicate the need in compelling language.

Security Is Everyone's Responsibility

If you are a staff user, follow the rules (and question the ones that might be unclear) and encourage fellow team members to do the same. You don't want to be Patient Zero of a criminal ransomware attack or the source of a hacker's exfiltration (aka theft) of company data.

Education strengthens you and protects you, your job, your team, your whole business (and livelihood). Make sure people on your team and in your division buy in and follow through with cyber security education, too. If no one has as yet organized cyber security education, go to the CISO and to the training manager in HR. Ask for it.

When you possess and deploy your individual level of education, you don't have to passively wait for the CISO's team or IT to detect an anomaly. Have team members in your unit hold a periodic cyber security meeting. Hold yourself and your team accountable to security — especially when talking to vendors and third-party companies. Are those vendors secure, too? Are your partners secure? Do you need to call in the CISO to help you determine this? Do so. It is part of his cyber risk assessment skill set.

Common Sense & Cyber Security Training

Cyber security training does not need to be highly technical for your staff or even for the executive suite. The technicalities and the details are for the CISO, other technology executives and all their technical staff members.

For staff users, cyber security training starts with common sense.

A first thrust must be to instill more awareness of risks in staff members who may have grown up from childhood with digitally connected devices. While this familiarity is an asset in the workplace, it is also a security risk. Why is that? When a person is long-accustomed to using an Internet-facing device or types of apps or doing types of transactions on mobile and connected devices, the less attentive he tends to be to the risks involved in using it.

In parallel, you may have the "Luddites" in the house who won't even carry a smartphone (very rare, I admit, but I have seen it more often than you can imagine). Train them, too, as their lack of familiarity and skill with devices, software, tech tools makes them a breach waiting to happen right alongside the younger savvy users.

Secondly, training and awareness about the most common data breaches is needed since roughly 90% of data breaches businesses experience are caused by human errors. They are caused by (and "error" implies that the employee did so inadvertently or through sleepy negligence rather than maliciously, so don't point fingers) the humans they employ.

Educate and illustrate the hackers' basic tools of spear phishing, social engineering, ransomware, and malware. Give real examples from the media of how hackers have manipulated employees to create an opening they immediately or later use to commit their crimes. Show real emails and other messaging that demonstrate phishing and social engineering to your staff. The CISO and/or their reports should be explaining to all staff how to use email securely. Email has been with us for 25 or more years and is ubiquitous in private life and in the workplace. It has become part of the environment we navigate, and that is just what makes it dangerous (as with texting/IM tools). It will be necessary to have some clear, hard and fast policies for using business email (sending with Cc and Bcc rules; receiving, opening, examining messages; storing/archiving). Have similar policies for IM and texting usage.

Also educate in what non-secure Wi-Fi connections are and how to take security measures. Using Bluetooth technology in public? What do your employees need to know about staying secure? And if any mobile devices or peripherals such as external hard drives or memory sticks go missing, make sure your staff treats such incidents just as they would with a stolen personal credit card or driver license: Report it immediately.

Explain to staff about levels of access and why they only have a certain level of access to company databases or functionalities. If they notice that their access has changed (either become more limited or suddenly more expanded), they must report this immediately.

Thirdly, show your staff how to set and securely remember strong passwords. From C-Suite to the mailroom, no one likes to remember a complex password, but *you must take this step* for cyber security. With no strong password, it is like living in the highest crime neighborhood of your city with no locks on the door and windows wide open day and night. We don't do it then; don't do it now. This is a front-line defense everyone hates to give attention to, and hackers take advantage of you. Don't let them.

Fourthly, any time you have skeleton crews — IT or any staff — be aware that it is not just employees who know that there is a potential weakness in the business. In times like COVID-19 many businesses are still operating on "essential staff only" in their usual offices, plants, and brick-and-mortar locations. But your business is also vulnerable at times when you are moving offices, installing a brand-new space, training a massive number of new hires (with no cyber security training just yet). Remember that a whole host of threat actors knows you are vulnerable and will try to use this as the perfect time to penetrate the light/nonexistent defenses you have in place. Make sure all staff are extra cautious in such circumstances.

Lastly, comfort your staff as you educate them. Don't point the finger at them as potential or past front-line cyber breach accomplices! Let them know they need not be a criminal's victim. Create willingness in all employees to immediately report or get CISO team support for any mysterious operations such as strange transactions or modifications to data; strange email or instant message; suspicious digital material or unusual transactions that come across their screens. This is just as acceptable as dialing 911 even if you are not sure that you need the police: Better safe than sorry. Make sure your staff understands that they can get tech support at any time suspicions arise.

Cyber security awareness needs to be about an absence of events, too. This sounds strange and hard to nail down, but if there are no incidents, that doesn't guarantee that nothing is going wrong or can go wrong. Make sure the CISO trains on this type of cyber security awareness as well. As the saying goes, "It was absolutely calm before all hell broke loose."

It Is Not Going Away

You have a cyber security program at a high maturity level. You have trained all staff and make a point to train newly on boarded staff in cybersecurity awareness and cyber security measures.

That's the good news.

The bad news is that such actions, implemented one time, will never be enough. You cannot rest on your laurels. Constantly devising new tools, new maneuvers, new entry points to get at your data. You must be as vigilant as they are relentless.

Cyber criminals are savvy about human emotions and human behaviors and continuously adjust their approaches to trick/convince (albeit from halfway around the world) employees to misplace or appropriate (aka steal) sensitive information for them. Largely, the employee does so innocently, accidently or through tired negligence of cyber security measures. Surveys determined that 28% of employees have uploaded a file containing sensitive data to the cloud. Make sure your policies also guide such storage practices.

Your CISO will tell you how frequently you need to upgrade your staff training. Your CISO will let C-suite and the board of directors know when your cyber security program needs upgrading, expanding, and strengthening. Listen to the CISO's recommendations. Put the budget and the time aside to implement them.

As a CISO continuously presenting persuasive reasons for ongoing training in cyber security measures, I am well aware that

C-suite is all too ready to cut any kind of training from the budget when things get tight. In case you have not been enumerating as you have been reading these pages the protective benefits of cyber security training, let me list them here for you again:

- protect revenue streams

- protect the business's and stakeholders' reputations

- keep your clients and customers feeling safe and loyal

- prevent disruptions to business operations

- prevent lawsuits

- protect your intellectual property (IP)

- protect customer and employee personal identification data

- protect data from vandalism, outright theft, being held hostage

Chapter 19

The Security Talent Gap — Cyber Is Where the Cool Kids Hang Out

W E HAVE SEEN IN THESE PAGES HOW NATION STATES are actively identifying and grooming young teens as hackers "for the benefit of the motherland". I have mentioned how the US military has internal red and blue hacker teams, and how the largest corporations likewise might employ in-house or contracted hackers to test the business's defenses and to bolster them as needed.

If you are an adult with younger children or older ones through the millennial generation, you know how easy it is for our younger generations to learn how to program their own apps (for both fun and profit) and other types of software, and (I have to say it) even do a little hacking out of curiosity. All nation states are doing is taking the natural curiosity and budding talent of this age group and nurturing it... and not always (rarely!) to your benefit.

Knowing what experts say about the "best practices in cyber security" is not enough. In your teams, divisions, business units and at all your locations, your job is to educate the non-tech staff you employ. Your job is to make sure your external partners' employees are also cyber security-aware and proactive in their own defenses.

Cyber Security Education & Training

You won't need IT professionals on every team, far from it. You will, however, need to know that everyone on all your teams is hyper-aware of the weak point each one might become if they do not all follow best practices. Encourage everyone up and down the hierarchy to become a cyber ambassador by 1) closing the security *talent* gap and 2) closing the security *education* gap.

What is a "cyber ambassador"? It is everyone being on breach alert. Everyone aware of what a hacking attempt looks like. It is talking about it with the same amount of attention each gives to his own function on the team and in the business. Have an agenda items at staff meetings about "cyber news", or what any of you see as risks in your own team. Don't count on IT to identify issues; you and all staff members should be the ones bringing issues to them.

Just as functional training of your staff improves employee engagement and your overall bottom line, so too can cyber security training improve your defenses in cyberspace. As I have said elsewhere, no one can be exempt from practicing good cyber defensiveness, not the top executives and not the external partners you do business with.

Additional to nurturing staff awareness, know that more and more it is your own end-users and customers who are pointing out cybersecurity weaknesses in your defensive structure. Listen to them. Investigate and act on what they tell you. Train your people to watch in those new directions for security weaknesses.

A recent consumer example: Using her personally devised password for access to her own online health insurance account, an insured individual was unexpectedly taken to an unknown physician's home page within the insurance system website. Listed right on the page that popped up for her on her home office computer was a list of three dozen or more unknown patients of that physician (presumably that the physician himself could see in the system using his own password). She immediately called the IT department of the health insurance provider and got bounced around a certain number of times in disbelief before she was actually taken seriously and connected to the IT director. Of course, the IT director was shocked, dismayed, and flummoxed. The real question for the IT director was: How many consumers looked through other private parties' "HIPAA-Protected" health records without reporting any kind of glitch? (The next question you should now have is: Did the CIO/CTO or IT director redirect this concern to the CISO or take care of it in IT? Hint: At best, you want a collaborative investigation into the matter and a decision between the two departments on the remedy to implement, and who implements it.)

Listen to your customers, customers, clients, employees, and external partners! Groom the next generation of employees in cyber security awareness. How? You have this opportunity if you are assigned as a mentor to any new hire in the business. But also do your part to groom the next generation of White Hats…

Grooming the Next Generation of Cool Kids (Cyber Warriors)

I've mentioned the White Hats and the Black Hats. Cybercriminal groups have not been waiting around for you to catch up but have been continuously recruiting black hats by the tens of thousands.

White hats — the good guys who know how to and do protect your business — seem harder to find. It is not an illusion. They are indeed harder to find. There is definitely a "labor shortage" in this field. Forbes estimates that by 2021 (which is right now, in recruitment terms) there will be a worldwide shortfall of 3.5 million qualified trained "security engineers" for business and industry, government and military. This comes to around 300,000 unfilled positions in the US alone.

Qualified technology staff, not to mention those who come to you already extensively and intensively trained in cyber security, measures are harder and harder to find. More specifically, among businesses surveyed by the Information Systems Security Association (ISSA) and independent industry analyst firm Enterprise Strategy Group (ESG) in 2018, cloud security personnel, application security staff and security analysis and investigations specialist positions went begging in about one third of organizations that were actively attempting to hire for them.

As you surely realize, no "warm body hiring" will fill this highly specialized gap. That means that cybercriminal groups, all those Black Hat hackers, are rubbing their hands together in glee because you are so vulnerable to them and their ever-evolving hacking tactics and tools.

The bottom line here? Your CISO and his cyber security team must be able and willing to train their own successors, mentor up-and-coming security and IT (or others that show promise and interest) entry level staff you already employ, and even become scouts out in the marketplace to find talent of interest.

This also explicitly calls for 1) a line item in your CISO's job description ("cyber security trainer") and 2) an explicitly broader training budget for this team. It's not good enough to pay those 6-figure salaries to your CISO and his team members, but you must also commit to a robust continuing education budget for them! This is crucial to keeping up with the cybercriminals' tactics and tools. If you are one of our corporations with a Corporate University, add this training program to your offer, and high-level teaching talent to the roster.

Another great source of talent to groom would be through your local university, college, or junior college. I highly recommend working with your HR team to start a cybersecurity internship program at your organization. These higher education institutions have a wealth of resources that are eager to learn from and be mentored by professionals already established in the field of cybersecurity. Though most of these highly skilled labor internships come with a salary, it is very budget friendly. The benefit is twofold, you get skilled and eager talent ready to be part of your team and you get a talent pipeline for hiring any future needs you may have.

Look Beyond Your Sector

As an Air Force veteran myself, I know the military talent of our armed forces veterans. It definitely includes cyber security know-how. Consider hiring these more mature, highly trained men and women to be part of your cyber security team, but also as those cyber security trainers and mentors your business calls for. If you do not have much comfort in directly hiring such former military into your private sector businesses, develop a paid internship program which rolls them onto your staff in a graduated manner. Find a way to sponsor or scholarship such individuals as they refresh, adapt, and upgrade their talent side-by-side with your current team.

If your corporation has an academic degree sponsorship/scholarship program which supports qualified employees in their pursuit of a Bachelor's degree or a Master's degree, consider adding financial support to those pursuing cybersecurity certifications and advanced training.

Likewise consider cross pollination, by which I mean that your corporation partners with similar sized businesses in very different industries to welcome in an exchange of cyber security personnel. The goal is to learn from how other industries have been addressing cyber security needs. Indeed, your own staff's solutions might benefit those other industries, just as those other industries can bring you tactics, techniques and solutions that work better than what you have been doing. Another version of this is to send your CISO and his most "aware" staff to another country in an exchange with a foreign like industry corporation; other cultures think differently than we do about many things including cybersecurity. At a minimum, your organization should encourage this type of networking within your industry and others.

As an example of this type of international sharing, the French national utility company EDF (Électricité de France) has done any number of international exchanges, including an exchange with one of the major electric utility businesses of Japan. The goal is to share strategy, infrastructure philosophies and … types of cyber security breaches each has faced and the respective defenses against them.

Cross pollinate. Large public and private organizations have been doing it for decades around the world at the C-suite level as well as at the specialist level.

A recent CSIS survey, called *Hacking the Skills Shortage*, polled IT decisionmakers across eight countries. It learned that 82% of employers are suffering a shortage of in-house cybersecurity know-how, and 71% feel that such a talent gap already causes and can lead to more damage to their organizations. Get creative to fill the gap.

Dive Deeper

This next bit of creative advice might sound a bit of a reach, but just as corporations go into universities to find future staff on Career Days, you should do what cybercriminals (think nation states) are already doing: Present or mentor at high schools and middle schools to source talent; at the very least it will be goodwill for your organization.

The way you can do that is twofold. The first approach is to go into the schools to educate the students on cybersecurity — tactics they can apply to their home computers and mobile devices and to their digital lives in general. The second approach is to talk about careers in information security, information technology, artificial intelligence, and machine-based learning. Don't be surprised at the wide interest you attract!

Consider that these younger children might also be scholarship material as you track them and train them throughout their remaining school years. Just as Master's and PhD candidates receive full scholarships from corporations and then "owe" a certain number of years of employment and to those organizations as a pay-it-forward system, so you can devise such programs for younger students in cooperation with their school district and their parents.

Such an example of this was brought to my attention. It happens outside information technology, but you can apply it: A PhD student in Clinical Psychology was awarded a full scholarship by the US Veterans Administration, in exchange for some years working in VA hospitals as resident psychologist. The VA was desperate for such mental health professionals; this approach closed the gap for them. How can you apply such a technique to your own needs?

Chapter 20

United as One

CYBER THREAT INTELLIGENCE GATHERING — AND SHARing it — is crucial to our individual, commercial, military, industrial and national security.

From Information to Intelligence

You must realize that cyber threat actors do not work only in isolation from each other but very often in collaboration with each other. To counter their criminality, we — the good guys, the white hats — must likewise not work in isolation from each other but more and more in collaboration. By working in collaboration with each other and pooling the information about potential or actual cyber threats that come to our direct attention, we can, as a cyber-aware nation, detect patterns in the threats. The more information we can collect and share, the more effective our preventative actions and post-breach remedies will be.

As we collect and share information, it transmutes itself into "intelligence". Just like the military or a government entity, this intelligence can help us understand cyberthreat actors, cyberthreat tactics and give us the "intel", as it were, to thwart them before they become an issue.

We must do this collaboratively, and as a nation of businesses, government and military entities and informed community leaders we have made a good start. Organizations in government such as Homeland Security's CISA (Cybersecurity and Infrastructure Security Agency) is one such, and it calls its process simply "Information Sharing and Awareness". That's Threat Intelligence, in a nutshell. And as a matter of curiosity, cyber intelligence has its own abbreviation within the greater intelligence community: CYBINT.

Don't Isolate

Cyber protection for your own business is all about collecting and acting on "threat intelligence" you have right at your fingertips. As discussed in these pages, when an employee discovers something suspicious in his digital transactions, he notifies the company's CISO.

When you agree to share this information beyond your walls with other organizations (private sector such as sister companies or peer companies in your industry; public sector such as the FBI), it becomes cyber intelligence. It is now cyber threat intelligence that can be acted upon to protect many more businesses than just your own. It is intel that can be used against your cyber enemies.

To find and collect "cyber threat intelligence", you might first look in your own house, so to speak — your own business entity and your own private home. You have been developing sharpened awareness of what cyber threats and cyber weaknesses look like. It is my hope that this book has helped you hone that awareness.

Alertness to threats, as well as sharing what those threats and vulnerabilities are, is how everyone can work together to identify and shut out cyber threats trying to take advantage (and hopefully, more and more rarely succeeding) of your valuable data, reputation, identity, intellectual property.

Come Together

Tighten up those vulnerabilities you see right at your desk and right on your own devices and within your own usage habits. But go further. Don't protect yourself in isolation. There is a growing number of industry and public/private groups focused solely on identifying cyber vulnerabilities across many types of systems and developing cyber defenses to tighten them up. As a CISO belonging to a number of such groups, I recommend that you assign someone at C-suite and board level to participate.

Threat intelligence, if we as a country full of cyber-vulnerable entities come together, can keep us secure. The goal is clear: Eliminate our cyber weak points while prioritizing cyber security programs within each organization, in view to reducing our exposure to threat actors and the resulting loss of assets.

COVID-19 has demonstrated to us all how a shutdown of service and product businesses, logistical businesses and manufacturing plants can adversely affect our way of life. Yet this scenario was not even about cyberattacks! Imagine if the economy had instead been victim to a similarly broad-based concerted attack from cyber criminals... The risks are real. Coming together to protect ourselves is the obvious response. As I've tried to say in many ways in these pages, cyber security is no longer the sole concern of professional technology people nor is conversation about cyber threats and cyber security reserved to professional meetups such as The RSA Conference (a renowned series of international cyber security conferences).

Beyond the business/home focus, there are free national resources for cyber-collaboration. One such among many others which welcomes members of the public, is InfraGard (https://www.infragard.org/). Along with other business executives, entrepreneurs, military and government officials, computer professionals, academia and state and local law enforcement professionals, you can join the InfraGard organization and make insightful contributions to our national cyber defenses. Your company's own CISO (like me), your CIO or CTO, any other executive or board member might be called upon to work with Homeland Security or collaborate with the FBI on investigations or cyber-defense-building projects.

Industries and sectors have formed collaborative groups focused on protecting each one's respective assets through threat intelligence gathering and sharing. One such group is the Financial Services Information Sharing and Analysis Center (FS-ISAC).

While not all US states are actively involved in cyber security programs at the local level (i.e.: counties and major metro areas), a number of states are collaborating with their cities and counties for cyber security information sharing and cyber security program creation. As just a few examples, Colorado launched the Colorado Threat Information Sharing (CTIS) network. Illinois created a Cyber Navigator Program in 2018 as a partnership between the Department of Innovation Technology and State Board of Elections. Indiana has its Cybersecurity Council. Iowa has leveraged funds offered by the State Homeland Security Grant Program to acquire cyber security licensing, appliances/hardware and tools for its 99 counties.

Nationally, our leaders are also paying attention. There is the Cybersecurity Moonshot project, hosted by the National Security Telecommunications Advisory Committee (NSTAC) whose objective is twofold: 1) move the power from attackers to defenders and regain user trust in cyberspace and 2) make the internet safe. It is, admittedly, a huge directive, a decades-long project to bring to culmination. Happily, it is built upon public/private collaboration — collecting information that becomes intel that can be analyzed and acted upon.

This is about information sharing on a voluntary basis. Opening up to "outsiders" in our competitive business environment can be challenging. Think, though, that cyber criminals are also … outsiders! You must welcome in the first so that the second don't get in.

A distrusting attitude towards your competition must be weighted to allow for collaboration amongst you to protect your whole industry. You are very likely to be part of a "critical infrastructure workforce" organization and need to share in order to stay cyber secure and (dare I say it?) open for business at all: Healthcare, medical and pharmaceuticals businesses; financial businesses; energy industry with its oil, gas, nuclear, electric grid management companies; transportation industry with its port and airport facilities; chemical businesses; agro-food industry and the related food distribution systems; water and dam systems; all manner of critical manufacturing enterprises…

There is some inequality or imbalance in various industries' cyber security preparedness. The transportation and energy sectors come to mind as not having made cybersecurity an integrated operational and strategic priority. Transportation is vulnerable to cyber threats through a shut-down of shipping ports or even our national borders through crypto-ransomware or a cyber-disruption in air traffic control. A story came to me recently (historic, mind you, not truly a recent cyber incident) about a military communications system failure/breach that allowed the enemy to know to the minute when fighter jets would have to rotate out of formation for refueling — and that is the one vulnerable moment the enemy struck. The energy sector, the pharma industry, the financial sector, and all others that are highly regulated need to be cognizant of how those regulations might block implementation of robust cyber defenses into your own most vulnerable areas.

Don't leave this to others. Participate. All levels of all our industries are vulnerable to some greater or lesser degree. Share intel. Get protected. We are all part of an economic web that mandates cooperation so that there is no proverbial weak link for cyber criminals to target.

Smart intelligent gathering is about getting information on threat actors, the intent of threat actors, and the actual capability of those threat actors to breach you. Threat intelligent analysis considers TTP's. Remember those? TTPS are the collection of tactics, techniques, and procedures used by threat actors, alongside their core motivations (ideological? monetary? disruptive? IP theft? ...) and their true ability to access the victims of their choice.

But We Operate a Cyber Security Program!

If a cyber security program is already in place in your company, chances are part of the program is the collection by real people and automated systems of cyber threat intelligence. Ask your CISO. The purpose of the intel is to support your cyber security program in its efforts to detect, prevent, respond. This intel helps you prioritize threats (for instance, when multiple reports come in on the same type of breach attempt) and the type of protective measures that need to be upgraded. As you analyze such intel, it can perhaps help you understand the nature, scope, and intention of cyberthreat actors.

When you formalize intelligence gathering, your security team and your executive management has more information. There are benefits to a focused collection of threat intelligence, such as revealing threat actors' motives or their decision-making processes. More intel can give your security teams advance notice (rather than after-the-fact notification) of potential threats so that they have time to build defenses. Cyber threat intelligence, however, your teams obtain it (in-house reporting; collaborative sharing with private/public organizations), can help the team reinforce preventative measures and show them what to watch out for system wide. Multi-sourced cyber threat intel can help your security team jump in sooner with preventative measures of all types and prioritize the greater threats with no time wasted.

Cyber threat intelligence sharing is all about acting in ever-widening circles of influence: from your own home and business, out to competitive/peer businesses in your industry, to your city and county infrastructures, to your state, regional and national partners.

Ransomware

*"I'd rather prepare and live freely than
be unprepared and live anxiously."*

—MARC CRUDGINGTON

*"There are no secrets to success. It is the result of preparation,
hard work, and learning from failure."*

—GENERAL COLIN POWELL

Ransomware — Texas & California Municipalities

AS SOMEONE THAT WAS RAISED IN TEXAS, AND NOW residing in Texas after being away for almost twenty years, this cyber-story grabbed my attention along with many other residents in Texas.

From the time the incident occurred it was the "smoke on the barbecue" for many Texas cybersecurity practitioners. We could not stop talking about it and subsequently tracking the incident. For me personally, I am good acquaintances with a person who was employed by the state of Texas in the Texas Department of Information Resources when this incident occurred, so I too followed closely.

Ransomware, as many may know, is a form of digital malware that encrypts files on computing devices from single personal computers, servers, and even networking devices. Because of its purpose — locking up computing systems so as to render them useless — cyber criminals use ransomware extensively in cyber-attacks. This is due to victims of ransomware attacks usually needing to pay a ransom (money) to the attacker to regain use of their computing system. Of course, this is in cases where the victim is unprepared and is willing to pay the ransom demand. The first occurrence of malware in the form of ransomware was observed in 1989 and the victims, mostly healthcare industry entities, were sent the malware by use of floppy disk — remember those?

Though many have needed to pay the ransom, law enforcement entities at the national and local levels advise against it, as do cybersecurity professionals. The reasoning here is that it feeds the explosion of ransomware activity: That is, if everyone pays, then cybercriminals quickly come to know this and multiply the ransom attacks in an out-of-control spiral of hacks as an "easy/ sure money-maker" for them.

The ransom money being paid can be used for many criminal activities from running drug operations to terrorism to state sponsored acquisitions of military arms. Also, there is no guarantee that once the victim pays the ransom, the criminals will provide the encryption key or even that the encryption key provided works.

The Cyber Edge Group, a well-known cybersecurity research firm, reported that in a 2020 report that 57.5% of victims surveyed paid a ransom and over 30% that paid the ransom were still not able to recover their data. Do you like those odds? Depending on the survey/report, the statistic can go up to and above 50% — still not great odds.

Isn't it best to just put that money to use in preparation? Ransomware against municipalities, schools, and businesses in general are rising year over year. A report from Kaspersky Labs stated that ransomware attacks against cities increased 60% in 2019 and that school districts are among the hardest hit. From Baltimore, MD, Florida cities, Atlanta, GA, Louisiana, and so many more across the globe, ransomware is a huge problem. What is worse, the attacks are turning into coordinated attacks.

That brings me back to the Texas incident which I believe is a classic case in preparing. It is reported that not one city in Texas paid the reported $2.5 million ransom affected by the ransomware malware strain Sodinokibi (REvil). The coordinated effort between the municipalities, state, and national governments and others was the result of a plan that Texas Department of Information Resources began to execute within hours of being notified.

The reports of ransomware began in the early morning hours of August 19th, 2019. Within four days, the state's response teams had visited all of the impacted entities. Just one week after the attack was reported, all cities had been given the green light to begin remediation and recovery efforts. Amanda Crawford, Executive Director, Texas Department of Information Resources stated, "It was this team effort along with advanced preparation that allowed a very critical situation to be resolved quickly and with minimal impact for Texans."

A list of Texas and United States government agencies involved in the response should be daunting to cybercriminals. We will not back down:

- Texas Department of Information Resources
- Texas Division of Emergency Management
- Texas Military Department
- The Texas A&M University System's Security Operations Center/Critical Incident Response Team
- Texas Department of Public Safety
- Computer Information Technology and Electronic Crime (CITEC) Unit
- Cybersecurity
- Intelligence and Counter Terrorism
- Texas Commission of Environmental Quality
- Texas Public Utility Commission
- Department of Homeland Security
- Federal Bureau of Investigation — Cyber
- Federal Emergency Management Agency

Nancy Rainosek, Chief Information Security Officer of Texas, Texas Department of Information Resources recommended, based on this particular incident, taking the following actions:

- Only allow authentication to remote access software from inside the provider's network

- Use two-factor authentication on remote administration tools and Virtual Private Network tunnels (VPNs) rather than remote desktop protocols (RDPs)

- Block inbound network traffic from Tor Exit Nodes (you recall that Tor is the only reliable search engine allowing access to registered users to the Dark Web)

- Block outbound network traffic to Pastebin

- Use Endpoint Detection and Response (EDR) to detect PowerShell (PS) running unusual processes

In addition to the above, other security practices to use to protect and recover from ransomware would include:

- Have a robust data backup strategy that encrypts the data; preferably separate from your network and with the data backup encryption and decryption keys separate from where the data is stored

- User awareness training about phishing, ransomware, and general cybersecurity should be done regularly to include phishing attack simulations

- Two-factor authentication should be required to access the stored backup data and for the administrator(s) to login to the backup system

- A sophisticated Endpoint Protection Platform (EPP)/ Endpoint Detection and Response (EDR) system that using artificial intelligence/machine learning should be on all endpoints throughout your infrastructure

- Block inbound traffic from country codes where you don't do business with (governments or private sector entities)

- Participate in threat intelligence services and threat sharing groups such as InfraGard or state and local groups

- Maintain a well-developed incident response strategy that includes coordination with external entities and test that plan frequently (no less than annual, prefer semi-annual or more if you can). Portions of the plan, such as testing file and computing system recovery could be done as part of IT Operations.

That might have taken you deeper into cyber-land than you wish to go. Sorry. This list is by no means not all encompassing and was just a taste of actions CISO and their teams might take. Each organization is different, but these best practices will go a long way in protecting you.

Lastly, to drive home the seriousness and escalating problem ransomware is, the week I wrote this case, I received two new reports about ransomware. The first incident involves the City of Santa Clarita, California, and its neighborhood called Newhall. The Newhall School District had to halt classes due to a ransomware attack. At this time, we are in the midst of the COVID-19 pandemic and all Newhall elementary school classes are being done online for the district's approximately 6,000 elementary students, and the breach is affecting all of the online learn for the district's 10 elementary schools. (Read more in the preceding chapters in this Part 4 on cybercriminals' motivations and rewards for targeting kids).

More troubling than the Newhall attack: Recently a hospital, University Hospital Dusseldorf, in Dusseldorf, Germany had a ransomware attack which directly contributed to the death of a patient. As reported, the attack was intended to go to Heinrich Heine University, but instead hit University Hospital Dusseldorf. Because the hospital's admittance systems were affected, the patient who required emergency treatment could not be/was not admitted. The patient was diverted to another hospital 32km away; the delay in treatment is what led to the patient's death.

Ransomware has increased in velocity and is increasing in sophistication. Ransomware is now being deployed with time bombs (not detonating until after a period of time) which may render backups ineffective. It can shutter the doors of a business, and if you are a larger corporation, can halt multinational business transactions and operations. If you were a small business that was attacked and were not prepared, could you afford (or, in clear: Could you keep the doors open if you had to pay) a six or seven figure payment?

Prepare, prepare, prepare...

PART FIVE

The Coming Cyber War

I F THE PAST IS ANY INDICATION OF THE FUTURE (AND I believe it definitely is), we will see a cyber arms race and cyber warfare that makes any past conventional arms race or war pale in comparison.

Even when casually analyzed against the past and present technological and cyber landscape, one can only conclude that escalation of cyber threats and attacks will increase in velocity and impact. The barrier to entry into cyberspace and to cyber weapons is much lower than that of conventional weapons — much, much lower. A few highly skilled developers or a little hard cash, or both, and any nation state or organized criminal group could acquire a cyber arsenal and proceed to cause disruptions to any infrastructure or organization on the globe they wish to target. We've seen this over and over again with many smaller ill-equipped countries — barely capable of causing harm in a physical war, they cause significant damage with their cyberattacks.

Often when CISOs and other cybersecurity and technology executives get together, we talk about the latest security systems available or the latest breach. Other topics are brought up such as the cybersecurity talent gap, Board dynamics, and how the latest current events (COVID or other) are impacting our organizations. It is rare that we talk about the future advancements in technology and the impact those are having and will have on our own cybersecurity programs and the country.

Though that mindset has shifted over the past few years due to the recent trends we see in cybersecurity, there is now a recognition of many in cybersecurity and in government that a new kind of warfare is here. It is my belief that those who ultimately rule in cyberspace will be the ones with the most significant advantage in conventional warfare as well. There are a number of megatrends developing that will have a significant impact on cybersecurity and how cyber is used both defensively and offensively.

Chapter 21

The Next Cyber Wave

"T OOL" IS, AS YOU KNOW, A GENERIC TERM. "CYBER tools", though, for someone like me (the good guy in the white hat who is performing cybersecurity for your business) are the specific protective measures we deploy to prevent breaches into your system.

What I would like you to remember is that the cybercriminals have their own sorts of "tools" which we cybersecurity good guys have named "TTP", for cybercriminals' *Tactics, Techniques, Procedures*. Those are the tools they use to fool you, breach your systems, and steal your valuable data assets from you. I talked about those in Part One.

In the next wave of cyber "tools" we must add the new technologies coming onto the market and already in some use, and which have started to create a certain amount of buzz . . . and havoc. Like the tools I just mentioned, such new technologies can be used for good. They can also be adapted by cybercriminals to do more of their nefarious bad works on your systems.

I'd like to keep the discussion of new technology simple. I will break it down into AI, Quantum Computing and Automation. Bear with me even if you start to sink into the geek-like details. It won't take long to understand what the future holds for us.

Artificial Intelligence

When discussing new developments in cybersecurity, not a conversation, conference, or article on the subject fails to mention Artificial Intelligence (commonly abbreviated as AI). You can ask ten different people to define artificial intelligence and you will get ten different answers. Ask the same person ten times and you may also get ten different answers. AI is one of those buzzwords, like Cloud, that have attracted marketing professionals like a moth to the flame. In its basic form and as defined by Britannica (and I paraphrase here), Artificial Intelligence is the ability of an internet-facing computer, computers, or computer-controlled robots to perform tasks which were formerly commonly associated with work only done by human beings.

Artificial intelligence is capable of doing mundane things like playing a game of chess. Think Alexa and Siri. Consider ultra-sophisticated tasks like learning how a human fully and completely interacts with a computer, then detecting the slightest change to that behavior to determine that something might be erroneous. Another such sophisticated task might be to spot a human through facial recognition software (we have read in recent media that municipalities are outlawing it as well as embracing it; it is a balancing act between individuals' personal freedom to move about and the needs of FLO — the forces of law and order).

Now you might say a human can continue to do these AI-assigned tasks just as well, but coupled with the enormity, speed, and accuracy of AI, humans can't compete. Thus, the attraction of AI.

As an example: Think of artificial intelligence in use at your Fortune 500 company correlating the activity of all employees. One of your employees logs in at an unusual time from an unusual IP address; that data is processed by a central system which then alerts your cybersecurity team (at your SOC or Security Operations Center) that something is suspicious; the team takes the predetermined action to find out if the log-in is indeed by a vetted employee or is a hack.

This activity is being done by a subset of AI called Machine Learning. Let's think about the human driver at a stop light. Envision that human is not from that city or even country, but from across the globe. The AI analysis is done in seconds. A bad guy has been located! Law enforcement from multiple agencies (local, national, and international) are alerted. That's both the future potential and the actual current power of AI.

But just as AI can be used for good, it can be used to do harm. Let's imagine, again at your Fortune 500 company, that a zero-day piece of malware was surreptitiously installed on an end user's workstation. Because that vetted user typically was known to make recurring visits to a particular (also approved) website, the site was infected by the malware and picked up by your employee. Network infection underway! The malware was silently in place but for now just doing some learning about the systems it is now embedded in and evading detection. The end user, your trusted employee, goes about his day with his usual list of tasks, using his usual software applications, emailing the usual people, and so on. Unbeknownst to them all, the malware has learned everyone's behaviors and has learned about all the software and all the systems you use. It is now propagated to every application server/computer touched and embedded in every email sent, embedding itself in each of those areas of your system and then diving further and further, deeper, and deeper. Still undetected! Now fast forward. Some months go by, and the malware reaches its "zero day", its D-Day for waking up. All of a sudden, based on learned behavior and a time lapse, the ransomware locks your company's infrastructure. Boom!! A cyber time-bomb called a ransomware attack, and that used AI to propagate, has just gone off in your business's systems.

Imagine the possibilities in the right and wrong hands with the power of AI. Don't just brace yourself for the impact or explosion. Prepare and protect yourself and your business from it in the first place.

Quantum Computing

This may be diving a bit into the weeds here, so bear with me. You need to know that quantum computing's promise has the capability to impact all industries across the globe.

Quantum computing is obviously expounding on the quantum theory and quantum physics — essentially the physics of how the nature of particles that make up matter and they interact with one another and is the underlying factor of how atoms function. Think of a windmill churning to create energy, how the water from a river can be harnessed to power a city, or how electrons can move throughout computer and electronic circuitry.

There is a lot of science behind this that we will not discuss, but when combined with other elements of physics — specifically the theory of relativity — the explanation is what happens when objects move very fast and creates quantum field theories. Einstein determined that the laws of physics are the same for all non-accelerating observers and that light travels the same speed no matter how fast the observer was traveling.

Computers that we use today rely on bits, electrical and optical streams that represent a one or a zero to operate; this is still what makes up our digital world. From downloading an application to watching a movie over the internet, it is all ones and zeros. Quantum computers use what is called qubits. Qubits are the quantum equivalent of a traditional bit when coded in quantum computing. Yes, they use a one or a zero, but quantum computing allows for the ability for ones and zeros to be used in a linear combination of both states; known as superposition. Yes, very heavy, and science-oriented stuff that I cannot do justice in explaining in a few short paragraphs, and so I will stop here.

Suffice it to say that how it impacts cybersecurity is through developments in quantum computing that allow computations to be *executed at speeds that will make today's supercomputers look like snails.*

> _My short message for you is this_: *With the coming quantum computing speeds, the foundations of cybersecurity — confidentiality, integrity, authentication, and non-repudiation — will essentially be in jeopardy.*

Because quantum computing is new in its development, it is hard to tell its full impact on our future. With greater computing speed, there will not just be "speed of lightening" breach risks to prevent, but also tremendous good. We'll see innovation in health sciences, better modeling related to finances, optimization of the flow of most anything including traffic, faster research to help solve many of the world's problems, and of course many beneficial innovations in cybersecurity.

The good of this is that we can develop new cryptographic techniques, new security defenses, faster behavior-based and machine-learning algorithms that can help defend against cybersecurity threats.

Automation

It goes without saying that automation has been around for decades and has helped gain efficiencies in many industries. Cybersecurity, being a relatively new field, is just now in its infancy of using automation to solve problems and threats faced on a daily basis. The impacts of automation on cybersecurity will only continue to increase as we find new ways to blend the use of technology into cybersecurity best practices to create efficient processes. We are already seeing many developments that achieving promising results.

Sophisticated cybersecurity tools have emerged since the mid-2010's that have helped fight cybersecurity threats. Some of those have been machine learning tools, as briefly mentioned, that quickly correlate events to determine if any are a threat. Automation allows cybersecurity teams to develop playbooks to take the results of many of these analytical tools and remediate the issue — thus shutting down threats. Now many of the issues are solved by the tool itself. Take a next-generation endpoint protection platform — a sophisticated anti-virus tool — that will combine threat intelligence, machine learning, and user behavior analytics to stop a threat. Automation tools can do the same things across a company's entire infrastructure.

Playbooks are being developed by users of these sophisticated tools to help stop specific types of attacks across a number of systems. Many of the tools used today are starting to incorporate or have already incorporated automation into them. As of this writing, SOAR (Security Orchestration, Automation, and Response) tools can be found as a stand-alone platform or incorporated in certain detection tools. These efficiencies help security analysts and cybersecurity teams quickly thwart an attack without human intervention or very little human participation.

Chapter 22

The Rise of Cyber
and Talent Development

ALLOW ME IN THIS CHAPTER NEAR THE END OF MY BOOK to repeat myself somewhat.

Despite honorable government efforts starting from the Clinton and moving through the Trump administrations, and despite the clear warnings about the risks posed when we are not attentive enough to cybersecurity threats, we still have not been able to solve all the issues posed to our nation, its structures and infrastructures, its organizations and its people.

This dilemma is due to many reasons. It takes just one vulnerability, just one opening, to create chaos in any entity's infrastructure. Many companies lack the required resources. In others, the risks are simply not taken as seriously as they should be. A new mindset around what constitute cyber risks and what type of cybersecurity measures are called for is starting to gain ground. Also, development of cyber talent is starting to be a focus by many government, educational, and private sector programs; there are partnerships being formed that collaboratively engage all sectors.

As discussed in previous sections, cybersecurity has gone beyond the ability of a traditional IT team to implement or keep up with. Cybersecurity has become one of the key risks that C-suites and Boards are finally becoming concerned about and starting to address — even though fully half of our private sector corporations are still lagging in preparation, talent recruitment and cyber security program development (much less implementation). But the trend is positive. It has to be, or "business as usual" will not be usual much longer.

As well, governments (and not just our own) have developed sophisticated cybersecurity forces in their militaries (you recall I told you about cyber Red and Blue Teams) and other crucial government agencies (where cyber White Hats are the good guys). We've seen an increase in these developments throughout the 2010's. While the government may have set the tone in previous years, the private sector across all industries and company sizes is also now on board. Most if not all agree (if not yet acting) about the reality and the costs of cyber threats and the need to have a robust cybersecurity program.

Companies are now beginning to expand the knowledge of Boards of Directors by either training their current Board members or including a Board member with a strong background in cybersecurity. More companies are also investing in a Chief Information Security Officer to lead their cybersecurity program... instead of assigning the role to the top technology executive. That individual, the CISO, must now fully integrated into the company's executive leadership team and participate as a contributing member of several key committees within an organization. No longer will any cybersecurity staff consist of a single individual on the Information Technology team managing a firewall. Sophisticated and larger companies have charged the CISO with building a robust and ever-evolving cybersecurity program that brings together the up-to-the-minute talents of multiple teams in a variety of disciplines.

Perhaps the greatest addition to the rise of cyber has been what we see in educational institutions. As a cybersecurity practitioner, this is a very exciting development that provides a lot of promise to our future. Universities and colleges across the globe are now offering Bachelors, Masters and Doctoral degrees in cybersecurity. Secondary education is also beginning to offer courses in cybersecurity or classes that touch upon cybersecurity. There are many private sector programs that include cybersecurity training as well. From formal university curricula to summer boot camps for your staff to online learning available to all at any age, cybersecurity learning opportunities are starting to blossom. Partnerships between corporations and higher education institutions have long been part of the collaborative landscape; now cybersecurity is part of the collaborations with internships and scholarship support helping to build the talent pipeline.

While recent developments in cybersecurity have been great and emerging technologies hold a great amount of promise for the future, our cybersecurity "chops" have not reached a level that is commensurate with the risks. Though survey after survey shows that cybersecurity is a key risk well at the top of a Board's and its C-suite's concerns, many companies still do not clearly identify the associated risks or take the CISO's reports and requests for support seriously.

Educating yourself and your staff is Job #1. Developing new up-and-coming Cyber Security talent ranks right there in that #1 spot as a tie! We want as many informed cybersecure staff as we pay — which is all of them! We want as many trained, talented, ethical good guys on our side as we can identify, recruit and train.

Chapter 23

What Everyone Should Know

IN THESE PAGES, I HAVE ATTEMPTED TO GIVE YOU A BIG Picture knowledge base from which to understand the major challenges to your business that relate to cyber threats. I've given you only a bird's eye view of the types of cyber problems we face.

In spite of this 50,000-foot approach I have taken, I hope you are getting the message that cyber breaches and insidious cyber risks to your data assets run are numerous, costly, business-devastating, daunting. I have found in my talks with individuals and groups that such a general picture of the threats — and a little paranoia — can go a long way to becoming aware, being willing to take protective measures and to be on the alert.

It's not enough to simply give up and be complacent. Believe me, as a practitioner, I understand the temptation. It can feel like an uphill battle when your business is one of those amassing Big Data. But there is too much at stake and this cause is worth a good fight. It is much better to be engaged and informed than check out and be dismissive about what needs to be solved. Ask yourself, if not you, then who? This is not something we can just pass to the next generation; it will be far too late by then. It requires our collective attention right now.

With a problem of such enormous proportions, there is much to do. Great problems require knowledge, national efforts, and global cooperation. We've seen a number of cybersecurity directives, laws, and entities formed to combat the growing number of cyber risks. A report from November 2018, submitted to the White House by the National Security Telecommunications Advisory Committee (NSTAC), is a Cybersecurity Moonshot initiative. The report discusses how we can regain cyber-power over threat actors. Additionally, the Department of Homeland Security (DHS) has a Small Business Innovation Research (SBIR) Program designed to help small business innovate technologies including cybersecurity technologies. These collaborative efforts need to continue and grow in intensity.

A national privacy law is needed just as we have enacted certain cybersecurity laws and directives. This will help our country in two significant ways. One, it will allow every person and every entity in the country to sing from the same sheet of music. Right now, we have 50 states, not to mention territories, each with their own laws on the books (or none at all yet, though this is quickly changing) to maintain and enforce. This overhead does nothing but cause confusion and keep national interests on the sideline.

Additionally, legislation at the federal level would help businesses across all industries and of all sizes. The cost for a multi-state business to meet numerous compliance requirements and simply do the right thing by each state it operates in will only erode a company's bottom line. I understand that states may have differing opinions on how to accomplish this (and with all due respect to states' rights), but I don't think you'll find too many in Washington that would argue that the security and the privacy of citizens is of utmost importance. If the multi-nation European Union did it (and it has), so can the United States of America.

National efforts to further the development of cyber talent should be considered. Programs that develop the next generation should be broadly enacted and marketed throughout the country. Curricula could be developed and shared through our public education system and be adopted or adapted by the private educational groups. As a student progresses through the curriculum, the courses become more robust in material learned and detailed. These could be allowed to fulfill current science requirements in high school and additional courses be offered as electives. At the higher education level, universities, and colleges, could participate in a partnership with the government. The government could in return offer scholarships or tuition reimbursement if the student works in a cyber role within government; corporations could even invest in the program as well. This could be modeled similarly to our Peace Corps: A Cyber Peace Corps.

Global Cyber Peace

Speaking of peace, we need to do more globally to declare cyber peace or draw cyber lines when it comes to what is acceptable between nation states; a global cyber peace agreement is required. Globally we've agreed on many large other types of initiatives, from fighting world hunger to combatting climate change to doing joint space exploration. While it is clear that not everybody is all-in with such efforts, there is momentum and a recognition to solve these issues and take on these endeavors together. We have an international space station! I am optimistic with the right administrations in place around the globe, leaders that recognize the issue at hand, we can come together as a world of nations to solve this issue. Let's put Cyber Peace on the agenda.

If not? One mistake could cause catastrophic global damage. It could happen sooner than you care to imagine...

With every passing day, new corporate systems come online to transact between one another. In small and large businesses; in any industry or type of activity; in government, military, or the private sector — there is a massive variety and volume of valuable data that criminals will want to get their hands on. Just because you don't have a clue as to the first step, they take to monetize that data or how it is that they can hold entities hostage for a payday — cyber criminals are clued in. They are pros at it. Never shrug off a cyber criminal's interest in your data assets. Criminals will always know how to make piles of gold out of your zeros and ones.

Our investment in security systems, processes, and people needs to multiply to keep up with the growing threats. Shareholder value is no longer the only issue on the table for discussion. The viability of your business is clearly in jeopardy. One ransomware attack can shutter your business for good. If proper security practices are not in place, you are dead in the marketplace and your competition will race right over your carcass.

The Board, executive leadership teams, and company owners should recognize the severity of cyber risks and put the right people in place to help solve those issues. They should authorize them to build a cybersecurity program that is commensurate with the size of the company and the risks it faces. Unfortunately, the easiest part may be hiring that individual — a full-time CISO, a virtual CISO, or a third party that manages the security. The hardest part is continuously supporting them throughout the life of your business. It requires providing the CISO with the

resources (including the cash budget) to fulfill the mission; creating the right culture to ensure all employees take ownership of
cybersecurity best practices (including annual training sessions);
giving the CISO the right structure to ensure that your business
is (as) bulletproof (as possible).

The Board and executive leadership team should, to a person,
be engaged and take time to develop a professional relationship
with cybersecurity leadership. You should all interact throughout
the year and across departmental lines.

Boards and C-suite should recognize that combatting cybersecurity threats means that there is no final state — you have never
"arrived" at a state of total protection. Unfortunately, our world
is filled with cybercriminal groups and well-funded and highly
motivated cyber threat actors that want to keep attacking and
siphoning off every last bit of data you have to make their dollar.

Neither can a CISO and cybersecurity teams' rest. They must
train relentlessly, dive into their infrastructure to find vulnerable
systems and form coalitions that can help them to succeed and
continue to stay ahead. CISOs need to integrate themselves into
corporate culture and become your "inside man" who is the key
catalyst for change. CISOs at a minimum must never be afraid to
speak up when the risks creep (or shoot!) above the acceptable level.

The two questions we all should ask ourselves — personally,
as a corporate individual, or as a small business, as leaders of any
sort of organization or team — are

1) What do I find valuable?

For instance: What Intellectual Property? What data bases?
What personal/private identifying information about staff or
consumers or third parties? ...

2) Why is this important to me?

For instance: It represents a lawsuit waiting to happen; it represents sales revenue taken in or lost for good; it represents our business's Goodwill and our reputation with our consumers and other partners; it represents our ethics and values (to do things right)...

As mentioned before, you are more than just individual contributors. You are the first line of defense. You are the backbone of a nation. You are the head of household. You are a leader. In all those cases you have a mandate: Security and safety for all.

When it comes down to it, securing our nation from the latest and emerging cybersecurity threats requires us all to act in concert with one another. Governments should develop peace agreements between nations that choose to participate and vow to do the right thing. Government should mandate that and hold businesses to a higher standard of protecting citizens' data and preserving their privacy; even protecting shareholder value should be a mandate. Citizens should treat this matter as one of national security, for now and for the future.

We can no longer sit on the sidelines and expect someone else to take care of the problem. Act by calling your elected officials. Demand that school boards and state education officials not only add a cyber education to the curriculum but add a more robust cyber security system to their own networks to protect our children and our families. Hold businesses in possession of your private data accountable to its security. If you don't act, cybercriminals operating with no governance or boundaries in cyberspace will act at your peril.

Conclusion

Tomorrow Is Upon Us Today

THE CYBER WAR OF TOMORROW IS UPON US TODAY AND it has been for a while. You probably realized that as part of the previous Stuxnet write-up. That is how we have to approach this whole issue.

If we are being honest about the matter, it has been chipping away at our defenses for a long while. When we don't have cyber defenses or defenses that are not robust enough, the enemy walks right in and commits theft almost under our very noses.

Although in fact just at its beginnings (as costly as those beginnings have seemed), the rise of cyber warfare and the growth and increasing sophistication of cyber criminality is not of the future but is our "here and now". The need for robust cyber security programs and of ongoing training to develop cyber-specialist personnel will only continue to increase.

We must never be lulled by the volume of breaches into believing that "the risk and cost of breaches just comes with the fact of doing business". That might have been the mindset for our

20th retailers when talking about inventory theft and shoplifting statistics. Today, though, that attitude means you are letting go — giving up all your wealth, all your talent and all the value you create for countless consumers to the bad guys. Don't let it go at all. Fight! We have fought, certainly, but must continue to develop more talent and more tools to take the fight to the bad guys and win the cyber war that is upon us.

A 2018 study between Raytheon Corporation and The Ponemon Institute revealed that only 36% of the respondents felt that cybersecurity was a strategic priority for their leadership team. This is an alarming statistic given the major breaches we have witnessed over the past number of years. I also hope you will no longer be part of that small number after absorbing this information.

That statistic is also cause for concern since we know *unequivocally* that a mature (i.e. robust, ever-updated, ever-evolving) cybersecurity program can lessen the impact of a cybersecurity attack and even prevent most of them from happening. Cybersecurity and a strong cybersecurity program should be viewed as a business enabler — a risk reducer that allows a company to keep the innovation wheel in full motion.

The same study also pointed out that 68% of respondents' Boards of Directors are not engaged in the company's cybersecurity strategy. Directors lack briefings and details of how a company is mitigating cyber threats and protecting corporate assets and shareholder value. But when they do receive them, they must pay attention.

Could it be that these two statistics are the reasons why cybersecurity and technology teams are becoming more pessimistic about their ability to defend against sophisticated cyberattacks? They may also explain complaints that cybersecurity and technology teams lack resources, funding and the trained people needed to mitigate threats.

What's a Board to do, though? Keep throwing money at the problem? As stated in prior pages, this dilemma demonstrates the need for strong collaboration between the Board and the business's cybersecurity executive, the CISO: You must insist upon interactive conversation; shared learning; encouragement to ask technical questions in whatever language you possess and to hold firm until you get an answer that is not only clear, but detailed and complete. It demonstrates the ongoing need to develop and recruit cybersecurity talent for your organization; you might have to conduct that search on a daily basis to fill the positions, so do that. Such actions will help keep your organization and people safe from cyber threat actors and mature your cybersecurity program pragmatically.

Cyber warfare concerns are growing and the danger implicit in the above trends will, in the not so distant future, push countries into a conventional war or at a minimum a strong conventional retaliation. Just as the cyber talent dilemma is being addressed by those of us whose job it is to protect digital assets, have no doubt that our opponents are developing more and more highly trained cyber-criminals than we are developing cyber white hats.

Technology is in constant development mode on both sides of this cyber war. For the good guys, there is going to be much opportunity to do good with technology. For the bad guys, well, they will find many opportunities to use new technologies against us. It is going to be up to us how to tip the scales of cyber opportunity in our favor. It is our job as a society to continue pressing forward on these cyber issues to ensure that the good guys stay ahead of the bad guys and that more good is always done than harm.

Tomorrow Is Already Here Today for Our Adversaries

The cyber war is not coming. No. It is here — now! Yes, it is definitely already here. And has been here for a while as we have seen from past incidents.

Today is a memorable day for America, for all the wrong reasons: As I write this, it is 09/11 2020. It marks a day we will never forget. In the aftermath of those attacks — those very physical, devastating attacks — the spirit of America shined brightly with first responders and many others sacrificing so much including, for some, their lives. As I reminisce about the nearly 20 years since the 9/11 events, so much has changed — and we are in the midst of a pandemic involving of all things a virus (yes, medical, not cyber — but as a cyber guy the word "virus" is a trigger to heed!).

Over these couple of decades, technology and cybersecurity have changed at hyper speed and will not stop anytime soon. Thinking about the changes and the cyberattacks we have seen right in our local businesses as well as those affecting parties simultaneously across the globe, it is hard to not to conclude that the "Coming" Cyber War is already upon us.

Stuxnet was the first cyber weapon to cause damage in the real (physical) world as opposed to "just virtual damage", according to the Smithsonian. Many consider the Stuxnet to be the first cyber weapon. However, some would argue it was the coding "improvement" provided to the USSR for the Siberian Pipeline in 1982 and many more between the two; cyber warfare is happening more often than you realize. Cyberattacks such as performed via the Mirai malware, the Heartbleed bug, the NotPetya malware and the WannaCry ransomware will be more and more devastating on a global level. I won't name others that have crossed continental boundaries to devastate recipients/victims and caused billions of dollars in damage.

Stuxnet targeted Iranian enrichment facilities in 2009 and 2010 that set them back years in their efforts to become nuclear capable. Stuxnet destroyed centrifuges in Iranian facilities grinding them to a halt and rendering them useless. Cyber ransoms do similar business-halting damage to corporations of all sizes, in all industries/sectors and wherever on the planet they are active.

Stuxnet and the few global cyberattacks I have just named were not an anomaly — don't believe it. A review of the *Center for Strategic and International Studies (CSIS) Significant Cyber Incidents Since 2006* shows 49 pages of incidents. Do keep in mind that it is getting harder and harder for the organizations that do such things to maintain an exhaustive list of cyber-attacks.

These incidents on the CSIS list are not your run-of-the-mill "teenager in the basement" cyberattacks. They are large-scale incidents that have focused on governments, major defense contractors, global technology companies, and other sectors where losses ranged upwards of millions of US dollars. The victims range from New Zealand's stock exchange, Eastern European financial firms, US entities, the NSA, the Vatican, Pakistan, Turkey, China, Japan, Italy, Germany, the UK, Taiwan, Kuwait, Saudi Arabia, Israel, Australia, Vietnam, Philippines, Vietnam, Thailand... the list goes on. On the attack are Russia, China, Iran, North Korea, the United States, India, Turkey, and other nation state threat actors. It truly is mind-boggling to read this list (and I only made it through May 2020 on the list).

When you put the above breaches into context, it is countries attacking countries via cyber means. It seems like we are inching into a World War III. This is what nation state threat actors are. Cyber warriors. I believe we are only aware of the tip of the iceberg.

Ponder with me: This is cyberspace and it is, so far, much different from warfare with physical weapons such as bombs, missiles, planes, tanks, ships. I say "so far" because there has not been a human-life toll yet, or at least none that have been made public.

The lines between physical and cyber warfare are, however, becoming blurred. There is a shift happening, with the "talented" cybercriminal being hired as a nation-state "hired cyber-gun". Nation states are relentlessly attacking each other for data, intel, citizens' information, corporations' information. The difference between spy agency personnel and cyber-criminals has already begun to intersect, thus blurring the distinction between two.

According to the US Department of Homeland Security paper entitled *Commodification of Cyber Capabilities: A Grand Cyber Arms Bazaar*, both corporations and governments are facing the dilemma of emerging new threat actors; the paper further describes a grand cyber arms bazaar. Think of it this way: Imagine walking into your local grocery store and picking out any cyber weapon you wanted; it was developed and sold to you in your local store by some of the most sophisticated cyber criminals/hackers in the world. Now you make such purchases over the Dark Web but project into a future that even your child could go out and buy such tools off the shelf.

Imagine, too, hiring a group or creating your own to launch widescale attacks against other nations — just as today you would hire contract personnel to run your legitimate eCommerce business. It is already happening. Remember the Dark Web!

The balance of power shifts, and it is getting harder to keep up and maintain the old equilibrium and the former influence we had in the 20th century and even at the dawn of this millennium. A nation state threat actor no longer has to be a wealthy and sophisticated global military power to cause harm. Third world countries with small but specifically cyber-trained militaries can launch the same or similar attacks as any other country or entity when they have the relatively small amount of hard currency to shop in this "cyber bazaar".

The Coming Cyber War? Yes. Cyberspace has become a no-holds-barred war zone hidden under the cover of an intangible, ethereal, virtual world. Governments on every continent, including the US, are vying for the same type of supremacy a physical military power provides (but for how long?). Cyber weapons have moved to the top of the arsenal chain in every nation's armament to defend itself and cloak its secrets. All nations are in a race to claim an element of cyber superiority and the clear technical dominance that gives them.

As I look out at the cyber-horizon, I see great potential for us to collectively do good and make the choice to confront the cyber problems we face globally. If nothing is done, most assuredly we will see not just some vague looming "Coming Cyber War" sometime in our future, but one that is catastrophic in nature. We will have a real Cyber War thrust upon us, and much sooner and much more devastating to our way of life than we can even imagine (all due respect to sci-fi novelists and futurist screenwriters). Now we have a choice. Later we might not. Let's act now.

References, Resources & More Reading

Are We at (Cyber) War?

1. https://www.cedricleighton.com/about/

2. https://review42.com/how-many-emails-are-sent-per-day/

3. https://hostingfacts.com/internet-facts-stats/

4. https://www.statista.com/statistics/379046/worldwide-retail-e-commerce-sales/

5. https://www.csmonitor.com/USA/Military/2011/0307/The-new-cyber-arms-race

6. https://www.forbes.com/sites/louiscolumbus/2020/04/05/2020-roundup-of-cybersecurity-forecasts-and-market-estimates/#293618c3381d

7. https://www.darkreading.com/cloud/cloud-security-spend-set-to-reach-%24126b-by-2023/d/d-id/1334473

8. https://www.cisa.gov/about-cisa

9. https://www.poetryfoundation.org/poems/44272/the-road-not-taken

Cyber Warriors, Cyber Novices, and "Isn't this just a bunch of Star Wars stuff?"

1. Department of Homeland Security. https://www.dhs.gov/news/ 2014/02/12/remarks-secretary-homeland-security-jeh-johnson-white-house-cybersecurity-framework

2. Worst passwords ever. https://www.forbes.com/sites/daveywinder/ 2019/12/14/ranked-the-worlds-100-worst-passwords

3. More terrible passwords never to use. https://nordpass.com/blog/ top-worst-passwords-2019/

PART ONE: CYBER SPACE & THE CYBER WAR

Chapter 1: What Is Cyber Space?

1. National Institute of Standards and Technology or NIST is a non-regulatory government agency involved in cyber security framework development. https://csrc.nist.gov/glossary/term/cyberspace

2. Defense Technical Information Center is the repository for research and engineering information for the United States Department of Defense. https://apps.dtic.mil/dtic/tr/fulltext/u2/a589636.pdf

3. The Cybersecurity and Infrastructure Security Agency (CISA) leads the effort to enhance the security, resiliency and reliability of the USA's cybersecurity and communications infrastructure. https://www.cisa.gov/about-cisa

4. Cyberspace defined. https://en.wikipedia.org/wiki/Cyberspace and https://www.merriam-webster.com/dictionary/cyberspace

5. Cyberspace, as imagined by William Gibson the novelist. https://www.wired.com/2009/03/march-17-1948-william-gibson-father-of-cyberspace-2/

6. Cybernetics, art and cyberspace. https://web.archive.org/ web/20150826204717/http://www.kunstkritikk.com/kommentar/ the-reinvention-of-cyberspace/

7. Does government control the Internet? https://www.businessinsider. com/the-us-government-no-longer-controls-the-internet-2016-10#:~:text=The%20U.S.%20government%20finally%20 handed,almost%2020%20years%20of%20transition.

8. Who controls the internet? Harvard Business Review. https://hbr.org/2016/06/who-controls-the-internet

9. More on who controls the internet. https://www.iflscience.com/ technology/the-internet-is-actually-controlled-by-14-people-who-hold-7-secret-keys/

10. Internet vs Cyberspace. https://www.cybersecurityintelligence.com/ blog/the-difference-between-cyberspace-and-the-internet-2412.html

11. The WWW versus the Internet. https://www.webopedia.com/ DidYouKnow/Internet/Web_vs_Internet.asp

12. History of the Internet. https://www.internetsociety.org/internet/ history-internet/brief-history-internet/

13. Cyber ethics and cyber law. https://books.google.com/books? id=mE8NEL5JdmAC&lpg=PP2&dq=cyberethics&lr&pg=P-P2#v=onepage&q=cyberethics&f=false

14. What is the Deep Web? https://en.wikipedia.org/wiki/Deep_web

15. More on the Dark Web. https://consumerfed.org/consumer_info/ dark-web-monitoring-what-you-should-know/

16. Chief Security Officers (CSO) online hub. https://www.csoonline. com/article/3249765/what-is-the-dark-web-how-to-access-it-and-what-youll-find.html

17. The Consumer Federation of America, association of 300+ non-profit consumer organizations. https://consumerfed.org/ consumer_info/dark-web-monitoring-what-you-should-know/

18. Searchable news website about cyber security and intelligence. https://www.cybersecurityintelligence.com/blog/the-dark-web-what-it-is-and-how-it-works-2343.html

19. The dark web. https://www.techrepublic.com/article/dark-web-the-smart-persons-guide/

20. More on the dark web. https://us.norton.com/internetsecurity-privacy-is-the-dark-web-illegal.html

21. About cloud computing. https://www.cloudflare.com/learning/ cloud/what-is-the-cloud/

22. PC Magazine on cloud computing. https://www.pcmag.com/news/ what-is-cloud-computing

23. https://azure.microsoft.com/en-us/overview/what-is-the-cloud/

24. More on SaaS, PaaS, and IaaS. https://www.lifewire.com/what-is-cloud-computing-817770

25. Types of cloud. https://www.globaldots.com/blog/cloud-computing-types-of-cloud

26. Why use the cloud? https://blog.newcloudnetworks.com/the-top-10-use-cases-for-cloud-computing

27. More on using the cloud. https://solutionsreview.com/cloud-platforms/7-cloud-computing-use-cases-every-business-needs-to-consider/

Chapter 2: Cybercrime Is Global

1. A 2018 in-depth study of cybercrime, criminals and money. https://www.bromium.com/wp-content/uploads/2018/05/Into-the-Web-of-Profit_Bromium.pdf

2. The costs of breaches; how remote workers increase your risks of breach. IBM Corporation. https://www.ibm.com/security/digital-assets/cost-data-breach-report/#/

3. Chief Security Officers online. https://www.csoonline.com/article/3434601/what-is-the-cost-of-a-data-breach.html

4. Future costs of cybercrimes. https://cybersecurityventures.com/cybercrime-damages-6-trillion-by-2021/

5. Examples of cybercrime. https://www.exabeam.com/information-security/cyber-crime/

6. The FBI is active in cyber investigations, cyber tools. https://www.fbi.gov/investigate/cyber

7. https://www.digit.in/technology-guides/fasttrack-to-cyber-crime/the-12-types-of-cyber-crime.html

8. United Nations Office on Drugs and Crime. https://www.unodc.org/e4j/en/cybercrime/module-13/key-issues/cyber-organized-crime-activities.html

9. Source, both images in the chapter. https://www.ibm.com/security/digital-assets/cost-data-breach-report/#/

Chapter 3: Hackers & Other Cyber Criminals

1. Cyber threat actors. https://www.cisecurity.org/spotlight/
   cybersecurity-spotlight-cyber-threat-actors/

2. https://www.crowdstrike.com/resources/
   reports/2020-crowdstrike-global-threat-report/

3. A source for reports on cyberattacks and target types.
   https://www.sentinelone.com/blog/threat-actor-basics-understanding-
   5-main-threat-types/

4. The Department of Homeland Security looks at nation state threat
   actors. https://www.dhs.gov/sites/default/files/publications/ia/ia_
   geopolitical-impact-cyber-threats-nation-state-actors.pdf

5. The SANS Institute unites 165,000 cyber security professionals
   from around the world; read their reports on threat actors.
   https://www.sans.org/reading-room/whitepapers/analyst/
   top-attacks-threat-report-39520

6. Threat actors. https://www.crowdstrike.com/blog/meet-the-
   adversaries/

7. Advanced Persistent Threat actors. https://www.fireeye.com/current-
   threats/apt-groups.html

8. More on Advanced Persistent Threat Actors. https://content.fireeye.
   com/apt-41/rpt-apt41/

9. Hacktivism. https://www.pandasecurity.com/mediacenter/
   technology/what-is-hacktivism/

10. Hacktivism basics and history. https://www.trendmicro.com/vinfo/
    pl/security/news/cyberattacks/hacktivism-101-a-brief-history-of-
    notable-incidents

11. Hacktivism and businesses. https://www.sentinelone.com/blog/
    what-is-hacktivism-and-why-should-enterprise-care/

12. Stanford University on hacktivism. https://cs.stanford.edu/people/
    eroberts/cs181/projects/2010-11/Hacktivism/what.html

13. Hacktivist tactics 2020. https://www.darkreading.com/
    the-state-of-hacktivism-in-2020-/d/d-id/1338382

Chapter 4: Threat Actors Are Everywhere

1. ZDNet is a business technology news website published by CBS Interactive along with TechRepublic, with 35+ million readers worldwide. https://www.zdnet.com/article/cybercrime-and-cyber-war-a-spotters-guide-to-the-groups-that-are-out-to-get-you/

2. Top cybercrimes and cyber frauds. https://www.buguroo.com/en/blog/the-worlds-top-3-cybercrime-and-online-fraud-hotspots

3. Advanced Persistent Threats. https://www.fireeye.com/current-threats/apt-groups.html

4. Links to top cyber threat and cyber security reports. https://www.fireeye.com/current-threats/annual-threat-report.html

5. Who is Anonymous? https://en.wikipedia.org/wiki/Anonymous_(group)

6. Federation of American Scientists, cyber warfare and cyberterrorism; from 2015 but a very educational read. https://fas.org/sgp/crs/natsec/R43955.pdf

7. US Department of Defense's Cyber Warriors. https://www.fifthdomain.com/workforce/career/2017/07/25/heres-how-dod-organizes-its-cyber-warriors/

8. Some nations with cyber warfare military units. https://en.wikipedia.org/wiki/List_of_cyber_warfare_forces

9. Red and Blue teams. https://purplesec.us/red-team-vs-blue-team-cyber security/

10. Stuxnet event. https://en.wikipedia.org/wiki/Stuxnet

11. What is a cyber warrior? https://www.techopedia.com/definition/28615/cyber-warrior

From the Desk of a CISO: Stuxnet

1. The Stuxnet Incident at the Iranian Natanz Enrichment Plant

2. Book — Countdown to Zero Day: Stuxnet and the Launch of the World's First Digital Weapon, Kim Zetter, 2014. (https://www.amazon.com/Countdown-Zero-Day-Stuxnet-Digital/dp/0770436196)

3. Israeli video on Stuxnet. https://www.telegraph.co.uk/news/worldnews/middleeast/israel/8326387/Israel-video-shows-Stuxnet-as-one-of-its-successes.html

4. Pre/post Stuxnet. https://www.wired.com/2014/11/countdown-to-zero-day-stuxnet/

5. An "in the weeds" discussion about Stuxnet, and other malware pre/post Stuxnet. https://www.darkreading.com/threat-intelligence/new-twist-in-the-stuxnet-story/d/d-id/1334511

6. The Stuxnet attack. https://www.smithsonianmag.com/history/richard-clarke-on-who-was-behind-the-stuxnet-attack-160630516/

7. Background on Stuxnet. https://www.csoonline.com/article/3218104/what-is-stuxnet-who-created-it-and-how-does-it-work.html

8. 2012 article; history and development of the Stuxnet virus. https://arstechnica.com/tech-policy/2012/06/confirmed-us-israel-created-stuxnet-lost-control-of-it/

9. Israeli Ministry of Foreign Affairs website; about Lt. Gen. Ashkenazi. http://www.israel.org/MFA/AboutIsrael/State/Personalities/Pages/Gaby%20Ashkenazi.aspx

10. Article on the Siberian Pipeline Explosion https://unredacted.com/2013/04/26/agent-farewell-and-the-siberian-pipeline-explosion/

11. CIA article/document on Soviet dependency on western help for oil discovery https://www.cia.gov/library/readingroom/docs/19820921.pdf

PART TWO: Business Executives

Chapter 5: Data Is The New Gold

1. How much data we possess. https://europeansting.com/2020/07/30/data-is-the-new-gold-this-is-how-it-can-benefit-everyone-while-harming-no-one/

2. Value of your data. https://www.wired.com/insights/2013/02/is-big-data-the-new-black-gold/ and https://www.ibm.com/blogs/nordic-msp/data-new-gold-therefore-protect/ and https://www.rsm.global/insights/cybersecurity/the-value-of-data

3. Free trade of data; cybersecurity regulations. https://scholarship.law.wm.edu/cgi/viewcontent.cgi?article=1164&context=wmblr

4. World Economic Forum; how one event can accelerate dangers to and usage of data. https://www.weforum.org/agenda/2020/07/how-covid-19-ended-the-information-era-and-ushered-in-the-age-of-insight

5. Forbes Finance Council on data as the new gold. https://www.forbes.com/sites/forbesfinancecouncil/2020/06/18/information-is-the-new-gold/#53802260531a

6. Data usage vs data protection. https://www2.deloitte.com/us/en/pages/technology-media-and-telecommunications/articles/striking-a-balance-between-extracting-value-and-exposing-your-data-to-the-bad-guys.html

Chapter 6: Waking Up to See Yourself on the Front Page of the Wall Street Journal

1. Wall Street Journal; data breaches. https://www.wsj.com/articles/data-breaches-elicit-calls-for-more-transparency-11568280601

2. Wall Street Journal; data breaches. https://www.wsj.com/articles/marriott-reveals-breach-that-exposed-data-of-up-to-5-2-million-customers-11585686590

3. Wall Street Journal; data breaches. https://www.wsj.com/articles/new-york-regulator-charges-first-american-over-2019-data-breach-11595423988

4. Bloomberg News; data breaches. https://www.bloomberg.com/news/features/2017-09-29/the-equifax-hack-has-all-the-hallmarks-of-state-sponsored-pros

5. Center for Strategic and International Studies (CSIS). https://www.csis.org/programs/technology-policy-program/significant-cyber-incidents and https://csis-website-prod.s3.amazonaws.com/s3fs-public/200727_Cyber_Attacks.pdf

6. Nation state actors and breaches. https://futuretodayinstitute.com/trend/security/state-sponsored-security-breaches/

7. Cyber Security Daily News; Equifax breach. https://www.csoonline.com/article/3444488/equifax-data-breach-faq-what-happened-who-was-affected-what-was-the-impact.html

8. Krebs Security; First American Financial breach. https://krebsonsecurity.com/2019/05/first-american-financial-corp-leaked-hundreds-of-millions-of-title-insurance-records/

9. SEC; First American Financial breach. https://digitalguardian.com/blog/sec-looking-first-american-breach

10. California legislation. https://www.clarip.com/data-privacy/california-consumer-privacy-act-fines/

11. California legislation and fines. https://www.forbes.com/sites/forbestechcouncil/2020/05/28/ccpa-fines-fraud-and-fragmented-data/#490d922140ce

12. Breaches of government agencies. https://www.nextgov.com/cybersecurity/2019/05/cyber-espionage-targeting-public-sector-rose-168-2018/156849/

13. The Collection #1 Breach. https://en.wikipedia.org/wiki/Collection_No._1

14. CEOs in jail; what regulators say. https://www.forbes.com/sites/bobzukis/2019/04/10/regulators-want-ceos-to-go-to-jail-for-cyber-failings-should-you/#1904e2ed19fa

    and https://www.theverge.com/2019/6/29/20056655/jun-ying-equifax-breach-jail-time-insider-trading-department-of-justice

    and https://www.wired.com/insights/2014/05/ceo-takes-fall-information-security/

Chapter 7: Not Just Your Reputation or Raw Data at Stake

1. Identity Theft Resource Center. https://www.idtheftcenter.org/

2. Closure rate after a breach. https://cybersecurityventures.com/60-percent-of-small-companies-close-within-6-months-of-being-hacked/

3. The top Internet of Things devices at this writing. https://www.datamation.com/mobile-wireless/75-top-iot-devices-1.html

4. Important read on IoT devices and cyberattacks. https://wire19.com/warning-iot-devices-at-risk/

5. Medical devices at risk. https://www.medtechdive.com/news/coronavirus-chaos-ripe-for-hackers-to-exploit-medical-device-vulnerabilitie/575717/

6. Medical devices at risk. https://www.cnn.com/2019/10/02/health/fda-medical-devices-hackers-trnd/index.html

7. Cyber security and the CISO vs Plant Security and the CSO. http://cchs.auburn.edu/_files/isma-survey-paper.pdf

8. C-suite. https://www.dizzion.com/resource/blog/
    why-the-entire-c-suite-should-care-about-cybersecurity/

9. C-suite. https://cybersecurity.cioreview.com/cxoinsight/why-
    the-csuite-must-embrace-cybersecurity-nid-24164-cid-145.html

10. Cybersecurity and your job insecurity. https://www.darkreading.
    com/security-management/data-breaches-costing-more-c-level-exec-
    utives-their-jobs/a/d-id/746124?&

11. Cost of cyberattacks to global and US businesses. https://www.
    whitehouse.gov/wp-content/uploads/2018/02/The-Cost-of-
    Malicious-Cyber-Activity-to-the-U.S.-Economy.pdf

12. Background on CISO functions and role. https://www.csoonline.com/
    article/2122505/what-is-a-cso-understanding-the-critical-chief-
    security-officer-role.html

Chapter 8: Are You in Charge or is Your CISO?

1. What is a CISO? https://www.zdnet.com/article/what-is-a-ciso-
    everything-you-need-to-know-about-the-chief-information-
    security-officer/

2. Management role of a CISO. https://www.westmonroepartners.com/
    perspectives/in-brief/the-importance-of-a-ciso

3. Need for continuous CISO training. https://www.securitymagazine.
    com/articles/91653-the-changing-role-of-the-ciso

4. C-suite's cyber responsibility. https://www.forbes.com/sites/
    forbestechcouncil/2018/06/26/ceos-the-data-breach-is-your-
    fault/#3d97356658b0

5. Cybersecurity is an all-C-suite responsibility. https://cybersecurity.
    cioreview.com/cxoinsight/why-the-csuite-must-embrace-cybersecurity-
    nid-24164-cid-145.html

6. CISO traits. https://www.forbes.com/sites/forbestechcouncil/2018/
    09/24/ciso-should-stand-for-chief-influence-security-officer/
    #5fd9b939198f

7. Physical vs digital security. https://www.securityinfowatch.com/
    security-executives/article/21081306/who-is-in-charge-your-cso-or-ciso

8. Need for a CISO in C-suite. https://securityintelligence.com/
    where-the-ciso-should-sit-on-the-security-org-chart-and-why-it-
    matters/

9. Policy: Physical vs digital security. https://www.securityinfowatch.com/perimeter-security/physical-hardening/article/12337447/cso-or-ciso-who-makes-security-policy

10. Need for a CISO in C-suite. https://www.westmonroepartners.com/perspectives/in-brief/the-importance-of-a-ciso

11. Steve Moore Exabeam. https://www.scmagazine.com/home/opinion/the-role-of-the-ciso-during-a-cyber-crisis/.

12. Summary of the role of a CISO. https://www.zdnet.com/article/what-is-a-ciso-everything-you-need-to-know-about-the-chief-information-security-officer/

13. CISO preparedness. https://www.zdnet.com/video/under-half-of-cisos-are-ready-to-respond-to-a-cyberattack/

Chapter 9: Lessons Learned–Alarming Trends

1. Better C-Suite and boardroom discussions on cybersecurity. https://www.forbes.com/sites/forbestechcouncil/2018/12/17/cybersecurity-101-for-the-c-suite-and-board-members/#33ff630d5603

2. The NACD handbook to guide your cyber-conversations: The National Association of Corporate Directors (NACD) Cyber Handbook_022020.

From the Desk of a CISO: Target Corporation

1. The various news stories covering the massive Target Corporation data breach:

2. https://www.washingtonpost.com/business/economy/target-says-70-million-customers-were-hit-by-dec-data-breach-more-than-first-reported/2014/01/10/0ada1026-79fe-11e3-8963-b4b654bcc9b2_story.html

3. https://www.securityweek.com/targets-data-breach-commercialization-apt

4. https://www.darkreading.com/attacks-and-breaches/target-ignored-data-breach-alarms/d/d-id/1127712?page_number=1

5. https://www.startribune.com/march-11-security-firm-says-target-was-easy-target/249329741/

6. https://www.zdnet.com/article/anatomy-of-the-target-data-breach-missed-opportunities-and-lessons-learned/

7. https://www.bankinfosecurity.com/target-breach-by-numbers-a-7205

8. https://www.cio.com/article/2600345/11-steps-attackers-took-to-crack-target.html

9. The Citadel malware used in the Target breach. https://www.cyber.nj.gov/threat-center/threat-profiles/trojan-variants/citadel

10. https://aroundcyber.files.wordpress.com/2014/09/aorato-target-report.pdf

11. https://securityintelligence.com/target-breach-protect-against-similar-attacks-retailers/

PART THREE: THE BOARD OF DIRECTORS

Chapter 10: Why You Are Needed Now More Than Ever

1. Resources from the NACD, the National Association of Corporate Directors, are rich in cyber security education.

   https://www.nacdonline.org/insights/resource_center.cfm?ItemNumber=20789 and

   Preparing the Board for the Digital Frontier: https://www.nacdonline.org/insights/publications.cfm?ItemNumber=68348

2. Awareness for board directors. https://www.bitsight.com/blog/what-boards-of-directors-are-missing-about-cybersecurity

3. Detailed paper on a Board's 21st century role in cyber security. https://www.spencerstuart.com/-/media/pdf-files/research-and-insight-pdfs/cybersecurity_010516.pdf

4. Forbes Tech Council; cyber 101 for the board and C-suite. https://www.forbes.com/sites/forbestechcouncil/2018/12/17/cybersecurity-101-for-the-c-suite-and-board-members/#38a62a685603

5. White paper; your security-conscious Board. https://www.fireeye.com/offers/rpt-secure-the-board-room.html

6. Grant Thornton LLC, accounting and advisory organization; cyber security/Board white paper. https://www.grantthornton.

co.uk/globalassets/1.-member-firms/united-kingdom/pdf/documents/cyber security-the-board-report.pdf

7. IBM white paper; C-suite and the Board on cyber security issues. https://www.ibm.com/downloads/cas/M94RB4WR

8. https://www.herjavecgroup.com/wp-content/uploads/2018/12/ CV-HG-2019-Official-Annual-Cybercrime-Report.pdf

9. https://cybersecurityventures.com/cybersecurity-ceo-every-publicly-traded-company-needs-security-on-board/

10. McKinsey and Company, global management consulting; move your Board into the cyber 21st century. https://www. mckinsey.com/business-functions/mckinsey-digital/our-insights/ adapting-your-board-to-the-digital-age#

Chapter 11: So That's What a CISO Looks Like

1. MobileIron survey data. https://www.digitaluppercut.com/2020/ 06/the-c-suite-cybersecurity-risk/

2. C-suite as a risk to cyber security. https://www.mobileiron.com/en/ resources-library/surveys-and-studies/trouble-at-the-top-study

3. Profile of a CISO. https://securityintelligence.com/the-expanding-role-of-the-ciso-seven-attributes-of-a-successful-security-leader/

4. CISO on the Org chart. https://www.securitymagazine.com/ articles/90178-how-to-properly-position-the-ciso-for-success

5. More profile of a CISO. https://www2.deloitte.com/content/dam/ insights/us/articles/ciso-next-generation-strategic-security-organization/DR19_TheNewCISO.pdf

6. Qualities of today's CISO. https://www.pwc.com/us/en/services/ consulting/cybersecurity/evolution-of-ciso.html

7. CISOs vis a vis other C-suite executives. https://www.cpomagazine. com/cyber security/how-cybersecurity-leaders-can-best-navigate-the-c-suite/

8. CISOs vis-à-vis Board of Directors. https://www.acscenter.org/blog/ why-the-ciso/ciso-perspective-should-matter-to-corporate-boards/

9. Charts in this chapter. https://www.pwc.com/us/en/services/con-sulting/cybersecurity/evolution-of-ciso.html

and https://www2.deloitte.com/content/dam/insights/us/articles/ciso-next-generation-strategic-security-organization/DR19_TheNewCISO.pdf

and https://www.isc2.org/-/media/Files/Research/GISWS-Archive/GISWS-2015.ashx?la=en&hash=6D7686173046E0AD6DF6D-D9671E96035140A1C24

Chapter 12: Your CISO — CTO, CIO, or IT Exec, Team

1. How to staff for cyber security. https://www.nuharborsecurity.com/information-security-staffing-guide

2. ISC2 white paper; building cyber security teams. https://www.isc2.org/-/media/ISC2/Research/2019-Cybersecurity-Workforce-Study/ISC2-Cybersecurity-Workforce-Study-2019

3. Cyber security questions C-suite asks CISO. https://www.bdo.com/getattachment/c97be460-0786-4e79-817b-68b994afa0dc/attachment.aspx?ADV_2020-Cybersecurity-Guidelines-for-C-Suite-Executives.pdf

4. CISO as top line executive. https://igguru.net/2019/03/12/ciso-the-c-level-executive-missing-from-your-board/

5. CISO or v-CISO? https://www.cdg.io/proactive-security-articles/ineffective-ciso-vs-v-CISO/

6. How to hire a virtual CISO. https://www.csoonline.com/article/3259926/what-is-a-virtual-ciso-when-and-how-to-hire-one.html

7. When to hire a v-CISO? https://securityledger.com/2019/02/four-signs-youre-ready-for-a-virtual-ciso/

8. Pro/Con of a v-CISO. https://searchsecurity.techtarget.com/answer/What-are-the-pros-and-cons-of-hiring-a-virtual-CISO

9. More on v-CISOs. https://www.helpnetsecurity.com/2020/06/08/virtual-ciso/

10. Verizon/Yahoo merger was compromised. https://www.cnbc.com/2017/03/14/verizon-sought-925-million-discount-for-yahoo-merger-got-350-million.html

11. Marriott breach. https://securityledger.com/2018/12/days-after-massive-breach-marriott-customers-await-details/

Chapter 13: A Cyber Security Program Explained

1. Build an effective cyber security program. https://www.infosecurity-magazine.com/opinions/building-cybersecurity-program/

2. More on building an effective security program. https://www.forbes.com/sites/forbestechcouncil/2019/03/22/building-an-effective-cybersecurity-program/#5896bea6185d

3. How Much Cyber Security Is Enough? CISCO analysis. https://www.cisco.com/c/dam/en/us/products/se/2019/10/Collateral/security-bottom-line-cybersecurity.pdf

4. CISCO Cybersecurity Report Series 2020; CISO Benchmark Study. https://www.cisco.com/c/dam/en/us/products/collateral/security/2020-ciso-benchmark-cybersecurity-series-feb-2020.pdf

5. https://www.cisco.com/c/dam/en/us/solutions/collateral/service-provider/value-at-stake.pdf

6. Cyber Hygiene. https://www.upguard.com/blog/cyber-hygiene

7. IBM study of "data leadership". https://www.ibm.com/thought-leadership/institute-business-value/c-suite-study

8. Reducing the impact of cyberattacks on businesses. https://www.grantthornton.co.uk/globalassets/1.-member-firms/united-kingdom/pdf/documents/cyber security-the-board-report.pdf

9. What is cyber security? https://searchsecurity.techtarget.com/definition/cybersecurity

10. The NIST model. https://www.nist.gov/topics/cybersecurity and https://www.nist.gov/cyberframework and https://www.nist.gov/programs-projects/nist-cybersecurity-iot-program

11. Maturity models. https://www.infosecurity-magazine.com/opinions/most-influential-frameworks-1-1-1/

12. Maturity models. https://preyproject.com/blog/en/cybersecurity-frameworks-101/

13. More on what cyber security is. https://www.forbes.com/sites/forbestechcouncil/2018/12/17/cybersecurity-101-for-the-c-suite-and-board-members/#14f438925603

14. Costs vs benefits of cyber security programs. https://www.cloudmask.com/blog/the-cost-of-data-security-are-cybersecurity-investments-worth-it

15. More on the metrics of cyber programs. https://medium.com/security-transformation-leadership/the-business-value-of-cybersecurity-2dcd2b3c1fe

Chapter 14: The CISO Has Our (the Board's) Attention–Now What?

1. CISOs communicating with stakeholders. https://www.cpomagazine.com/cyber security/how-cybersecurity-leaders-can-best-navigate-the-c-suite/

2. Board/CISO relationship. https://securityintelligence.com/five-ways-to-improve-the-ciso-board-relationship/

3. CISO communication/presentation skills. https://cisomag.eccouncil.org/ciso-communication/

4. More CISO communication/presentation skills. https://bricata.com/blog/ciso-communicate-board/

5. CISO evolving role and helping boards understand them. https://www.ey.com/Publication/vwLUAssets/ey-eacln-viewpoints-cisos-and-the-board/$FILE/ey-eacln-viewpoints-cisos-and-the-board.pdf

6. How CISOs can present at board meetings. https://www.helpnetsecurity.com/2019/06/13/ciso-board-reporting/

7. Price Waterhouse Coopers coaching series. https://www.pwc.com/us/en/services/governance-insights-center/library/executive-coaching-series/five-ways-chief-information-security-officers-can-stand-out.html, with the full Price Waterhouse Coopers pdf here:

    https://www.pwc.com/us/en/governance-insights-center/publications/assets/pwc-engaging-with-the-board-five-ways-for-ciso-to-stand-out.pdf

Chapter 15: The Governance Of Cyber–Find It Or They'll Find You

1. Look for the NACD Cyber Handbook, 2020, published jointly by the National Association of Corporate Directors (NACD) and the Internet Security Alliance (ISA). And available here: https://www.nacdonline.org/insights/publications.cfm?ItemNumber=67298

2. Cyber Risk Playbook for C-suite and Board of Directors. https://www.fireeye.com/offers/cyber-risk-playbook.html

3. Basic cyber security questions to answer about your business. https://www.tetradefense.com/cyber-risk-management/15-cyber security-questions-to-ask-for-c-suites/

4. White paper for board of directors — the components of cyber-security governance. https://www.dentons.com/~/media/PDFs/ Guides%20Reports%20and%20Whitepapers/cybersecurity-090115.pdf

Chapter 16: What Boards Are Doing Today

1. Cybersecurity guidelines for C-suite. https://warrenaverett.com/ insights/cybersecurity-for-executives/

2. Corporate governance & the CISO. https://www.forbes.com/sites/ robinferracone/2019/07/09/good-governance-do-boards-need-cyber security-experts/#228a28e41859

3. Corporate governance; Harvard Law Press. https://corpgov.law. harvard.edu/2018/03/31/cybersecurity-the-secs-wake-up-call-to-corporate-directors/

4. More on corporate governance; Harvard Law Press. https://corpgov. law.harvard.edu/2020/03/15/cybersecurity-an-evolving-governance-challenge/

5. Corporate governance. https://www.isaca.org/-/media/files/isacadp/ project/isaca/articles/journal/2019/volume-4/redefining-corporate-governance-for-better-cyberrisk-management_joa_eng_0719

6. Corporate governance; Center for Long-Term Cybersecurity; University of California at Berkeley. https://cltc.berkeley.edu/ wp-content/uploads/2020/01/Resilient-Governance-for-Boards-of-Directors-Report.pdf

7. Board of Directors; statistics and data about Board role in cybersecure enterprises. https://boardspan.com/users/0/library/the-board-s-role-in-cyber security

From the Desk of a CISO: Equifax Breach

Media on the Yahoo settlement and the Equifax breach:

1. https://www.nytimes.com/2019/01/23/business/dealbook/yahoo-cyber-security-settlement.html

2. https://www.csoonline.com/article/3444488/equifax-data-breach-faq-what-happened-who-was-affected-what-was-the-impact.html

3. https://www.epic.org/privacy/data-breach/equifax/

4. https://www.fbi.gov/news/stories/chinese-hackers-charged-in-equifax-breach-021020

Breach fallout affecting (or not) Equifax Directors:

5. https://www.marketwatch.com/story/equifax-board-members-re-elected-despite-massive-data-breach-2018-05-03

6. https://www.wsj.com/articles/equifax-directors-win-re-election-despite-concerns-about-breach-1525384254

7. https://www.ftc.gov/enforcement/cases-proceedings/refunds/equifax-data-breach-settlement

8. https://www.bsk.com/news-insights/board-directors-beware-potential-liability-in-data-breach-suit

PART FOUR: YOU

Chapter 17: Security At Home –You Family And Kids' Future Depend On It

1. Get a complex password; here is why. https://www.foxnews.com/tech/risk-of-passwords-being-exposed-is-on-the-rise-report-says

2. Great resources for home cybersecurity - https://us-cert.cisa.gov/home-and-business and

3. https://us-cert.cisa.gov/ncas/tips/ST15-002 and https://us-cert.cisa.gov/ncas/tips/ST15-003

4. More great home cybersecurity resources - https://www.dhs.gov/how-do-i/protect-myself-cyberattacks

5. https://www.wired.com/story/secure-your-wi-fi-router/

6. https://www.lifewire.com/how-to-hack-proof-your-wireless-router-2487654 and

7. https://dot.la/how-to-practice-cybersecurity-at-home-2645983355.html

8. https://www.ibtimes.com/your-ultimate-guide-cybersecurity-home-work-go-2818655

9. https://cipher.com/blog/10-personal-cyber security-tips-cyberaware/

10. https://www.protectseniorsonline.com/resources/cybersecurity-best-practices/

11. Kids' cyber privacy. https://www.consumer.ftc.gov/articles/0031-protecting-your-childs-privacy-online

12. More on kids' Cyber-privacy. https://www.consumer.ftc.gov/topics/protecting-kids-online

13. California elementary school data ransomed. https://scvnews.com/newhall-schools-put-virtual-lessons-on-hold-after-ransomware-attack/

14. https://www.mercurynews.com/computer-attack-disables-california-school-districts-system

15. Tips to help you secure schools' data. https://www.securityinfowatch.com/cybersecurity/information-security/breach-detection/article/21094128/6-tips-to-help-curb-school-cyber-attacks

Chapter 18: You Are More Than an Individual Contributor

1. Harvard Business Review; Coronavirus and hacking risks. https://hbr.org/2020/03/will-coronavirus-lead-to-more-cyberattacks

2. More on Coronavirus and hacking risks. https://staysafeonline.org/press-release/ncsa-encourages-coronavirus-vigilance/

3. Cyber security and a remote workforce. https://www.burkelaw.com/pressroom-news-397.html

4. Company-wide awareness. https://www.informationsecuritybuzz.com/articles/security-make-people-listen-take-action-protect-organization/

5. Cyber hygiene and security training. https://www.align.com/blog/6-reasons-why-businesses-need-cyber-security-awareness-training

6. More on cyber security training. https://www.onlinecomputers.com/2020/01/why-security-awareness-training-is-important-for-your-business/

and https://www.securitymagazine.com/articles/91515-article-headline

and https://resources.infosecinstitute.com/category/enterprise/
securityawareness/security-awareness-training/#gref

and https://www.itgovernance.eu/blog/en/your-employees-are-your-
biggest-cyber-security-threat

7. Employees as the human firewall. https://www.entrepreneur.com/
    article/340838

8. The human factor in cyber security. https://resources.infosecinstitute.
    com/category/enterprise/securityawareness/employee-security-
    threats/#gref

    and https://www.newcmi.com/blog/it-providers-london-it-company-
    the-human-factor

    and https://www.trendmicro.com/vinfo/fr/security/news/cybercrime-
    and-digital-threats/data-breaches-and-the-human-factor-are-
    employees-the-best-defense-or-the-weakest-links

Chapter 19: The Security Talent Gap — Cyber Is Where the Cool Kids Hang Out

1. A few good cyber security certification programs to consider, which
    are reasonably priced:

    - **Cisco Certified Network Associate (CCNA) Security:** network
      security infrastructure, threats and vulnerabilities, threat mitigation
      https://www.cisco.com/c/en/us/training-events/training-
      certifications/certifications/associate/ccna.html

    - **CompTIA Security+** – core knowledge needed for intermediate-
      level cybersecurity jobs - https://www.comptia.org/certifications/
      security

    - **Systems Security Certified Professional (SSCP):** Is an (ISC)2
      certification and teaches hands-on network security, systems
      administration, security engineering - https://www.isc2.org/
      Certifications/SSCP

    - **Computer Hacking Forensic Investigator (CHFI):** teaches
      forensic/analytical techniques to detect attacks/attempts, how
      to obtain evidence, tools for prevention of future attacks -
      https://www.eccouncil.org/programs/computer-hacking-
      forensic-investigator-chfi/

- **Certified Information Systems Security Professional (CISSP):** teaches a variety of information security topics in ten domains: a little more advanced - https://www.isc2.org/Certifications/CISSP

- **CSX Cybersecurity Fundamentals Certificate:** an ISACA certification great for building a foundation to get start in the field - https://www.isaca.org/training-and-events/cybersecurity

- **Information Systems Audit and Controls Association (ISACA):** A World leading organization that offers cybersecurity and information technology professions in the fields of security, governance, risk, and audit programs for lifetime learning https://www.isaca.org

- **International Information System Security Certification Consortium (ISC)²:** The World's Leading Cybersecurity Professional Organization - specializes in training and certifications for cybersecurity professionals - https://www.isc2.org/

2. CSIS, *Hacking the Skills Shortage* (Santa Clara, CA: McAfee, July 2016): https://www.mcafee.com/enterprise/en-us/assets/reports/rp-hacking-skills-shortage.pdf.

3. https://www.esg-global.com/esg-issa-research-report-2018? utm_campaign=Cybersecurity%202019&utm_source=slider

4. The talent gap. https://www.forbes.com/sites/forbestechcouncil/2018/08/09/the-cybersecurity-talent-gap-is-an-industry-crisis/#33bf8552a6b3

   and https://cybersecurity-magazine.com/the-talent-shortage-crisis-in-cyber security-and-how-to-overcome-it/

   and https://www.csis.org/analysis/cybersecurity-workforce-gap

   and https://www.mcafee.com/enterprise/en-us/assets/reports/rp-hacking-skills-shortage.pdf

5. Cause of talent shortage. https://securityboulevard.com/2019/10/why-the-cybersecurity-skills-shortage-is-a-real-nightmare/

6. https://www.nytimes.com/2018/11/07/business/the-mad-dash-to-find-a-cybersecurity-force.html

7. Cyber skills shortage. https://www.csoonline.com/article/3571734/the-cybersecurity-skills-shortage-is-getting-worse.html

8. The military veteran solution. https://www.csoonline.com/article/ 3535270/addressing-the-cybersecurity-workforce-shortage-by-training-veterans.html

   and https://niccs.us-cert.gov/training

   and https://niccs.us-cert.gov/formal-education/cybercorps-scholarship-service-sfs

9. Fixing the talent gap. https://hbr.org/2017/05/cybersecurity-has-a-serious-talent-shortage-heres-how-to-fix-it

Chapter 20: United as One

1. Information Sharing and Analysis Centers (ISACs). https://www.isacs.org/

   and https://www.nationalisacs.org/

2. NIST (National Institute of Security and Technology) publication on cyber threat information sharing. https://nvlpubs.nist.gov/nistpubs/ SpecialPublications/NIST.SP.800-150.pdf

3. Collaborative cyber threat intelligence and sharing. https://www.cisecurity.org/blog/what-is-cyber-threat-intelligence/

   and https://www.cisa.gov/information-sharing-and-awareness

   and https://www.thinkcsc.com/collaboration-is-the-future-of-cybersecurity/ and https://www.edgewise.net/blog/fostering-public-private-collaboration-on-cybersecurity

   and https://www.internetsociety.org/collaborativesecurity/

4. Examples of state / local collaborations. https://www.nga.org/ wp-content/uploads/2020/01/NASCIO_NGAStatesLocal Collaboration.pdf

5. More on threat intelligence. https://www.crowdstrike.com/ epp-101/threat-intelligence/

   and https://securityintelligence.com/what-are-the-different-types-of-cyberthreat-intelligence/

and https://www.tenable.com/blog/why-global-collaboration-is-key-to-effective-cyber-defense

6. Public-private cyber partnerships. https://www.cyberscoop.com/radio/reduce-cyber-threat-security-risk-public-private-partnerships-deloitte/

    and https://federalnewsnetwork.com/commentary/2019/04/protecting-our-infrastructure-demands-a-critical-public-private-partnership/

    and Intelligence for critical infrastructure businesses. https://www.cisa.gov/critical-infrastructure-sectors

From the Desk of a CISO: Ransomware

1. Preparation. https://www.awakenthegreatnesswithin.com/35-inspirational-quotes-on-preparation/

2. Background on ransomware for executives. https://www.zdnet.com/article/ransomware-an-executive-guide-to-one-of-the-biggest-menaces-on-the-web/

3. Victims paid a ransom; still couldn't decrypt their files. https://datarecovery.com/rd/half-ransomware-payments-resulted-decrypted-files/

4. Increase in government agency ransomware attacks. https://www.govtech.com/blogs/lohrmann-on-cybersecurity/2019-the-year-ransomware-targeted-state--local-governments.html

5. Increase in government agency ransomware attacks. https://securelist.com/story-of-the-year-2019-cities-under-ransomware-siege/95456/

6. https://statescoop.com/texas-ransomware-attack-nine-named-feds-respond/

7. Refusal to pay. https://thenextweb.com/security/2019/09/09/texas-says-no-to-ransom-demand-as-it-recovers-from-a-coordinated-ransomware-attack/

8. https://dir.texas.gov/View-About-DIR/Article-Detail.aspx?id=213

9. California elementary school ransomware attack. https://signalscv.com/2020/09/newhall-schools-put-virtual-lessons-on-hold-due-to-ransomware-attack/

10. More on the California elementary school ransomware attack. https://www.newsbreak.com/news/2061602936854/ransomware-attack-hits-newhall-schools-halting-online-classes

11. Hospital ransomware attack leads to patient death. https://www.hackread.com/ransomware-attack-on-hospital-causes-patient-death/

PART FIVE: THE COMING CYBER WAR

Chapter 21: The Next Cyber Wave

1. What is AI? https://www.britannica.com/technology/artificial-intelligence

2. https://www.raytheon.com/sites/default/files/2018-02/2018_Global_Cyber_Megatrends.pdf

3. Primer on quantum physics. https://www.newscientist.com/term/quantum-physics/

4. Quantum computing. https://www.technologyreview.com/2019/01/29/66141/what-is-quantum-computing/

5. More on quantum computing. https://www.quantum-inspire.com/kbase/what-is-a-qubit/

6. General relativity. https://www.space.com/17661-theory-general-relativity.html

Chapter 22: The Rise of Cyber and Talent Development

1. CSIS, *Hacking the Skills Shortage* (Santa Clara, CA: McAfee, July 2016): https://www.mcafee.com/enterprise/en-us/assets/reports/rp-hacking-skills-shortage.pdf.

2. Multiple perspectives on the talent shortage:

   https://www.forbes.com/sites/forbestechcouncil/2018/08/09/the-cybersecurity-talent-gap-is-an-industry-crisis/#33bf8552a6b3

   and https://cybersecurity-magazine.com/the-talent-shortage-crisis-in-cyber-security-and-how-to-overcome-it/

   and https://www.csis.org/analysis/cybersecurity-workforce-gap

and https://securityboulevard.com/2019/10/why-the-cybersecurity-skills-shortage-is-a-real-nightmare/

and https://www.nytimes.com/2018/11/07/business/the-mad-dash-to-find-a-cybersecurity-force.html

3.   State of the shortage, August 2020. https://www.csoonline.com/article/3571734/the-cybersecurity-skills-shortage-is-getting-worse.html

4.   I am a USAF Veteran; here is a solution. https://www.csoonline.com/article/3535270/addressing-the-cybersecurity-workforce-shortage-by-training-veterans.html

5.   Some good tips for recruitment. https://hbr.org/2017/05/cybersecurity-has-a-serious-talent-shortage-heres-how-to-fix-it

6.   Training background information. https://niccs.us-cert.gov/training and https://niccs.us-cert.gov/formal-education/cybercorps-scholarship-service-sfs

Chapter 23: What Everyone Should Know

1.   NSTAC Report to the President on a Cybersecurity Moonshot, November 14, 2018 https://www.cisa.gov/sites/default/files/publications/NSTAC_CyberMoonshotReport_508c.pdf

2.   DHS SBIR Program. https://www.dhs.gov/science-and-technology/sbir

Conclusion: Tomorrow Is Upon Us Today

1.   Public/private cyber partnerships. https://federalnewsnetwork.com/commentary/2019/04/protecting-our-infrastructure-demands-a-critical-public-private-partnership/

2.   Department of Homeland Security; small business research funding. https://www.dhs.gov/science-and-technology/sbir

3.   "World War C". Understanding nation-state threat actor motives. https://www.fireeye.com/content/dam/fireeye-www/global/en/current-threats/pdfs/fireeye-wwc-report.pdf

4.   List of cyber events around the world. https://csis-website-prod.s3.amazonaws.com/s3fs-public/200901_Significant_Cyber_Events_List.pdf

5. Smithsonian; computer viruses. https://www.smithsonianmag.com/science-nature/top-ten-most-destructive-computer-viruses-159542266/

6. Geopolitics and cyber warfare. https://www.dhs.gov/sites/default/files/publications/ia/ia_geopolitical-impact-cyber-threats-nation-state-actors.pdf

About the Author

MARC CRUDGINGTON is the Chief Information Security Officer (CISO) and Senior Vice President of Information Security for Woodforest National Bank; he joined Woodforest in August 2012.

Marc also is the Founder, CEO, and vCISO of CyberFore Systems, a cybersecurity consulting and services company located in the Houston, Texas area. Previously he owned small businesses in technology consulting, real estate, and adventure sports.

Prior to Woodforest, Marc worked for Advantage Sales and Marketing, KPMG, and Silicon Valley technology companies with leadership roles in IT and engineering.

Marc is a veteran of the United States Air Force, serving honorably from April 1992–April 1996. He held a Top-Secret clearance and performed duties in intelligence, computer operations, computer communications, and network communications.

Marc holds a Master of Business Administration degree with a focus on Technology and Strategy, from the University of California Irvine, Paul Merage School of Business. He earned his Bachelor of Business Management degree from the University of Phoenix.

Marc attended the FBI CISO Academy in March 2017. He holds a Secret Clearance and CDPSE, CRISC, Security+, PCIP, ISA, Scrum Master, and ITIL certifications; previously he held C|CISO, PMP, TOGAF, CISM and CISA certifications.

Marc is a member of the Private Directors Association. He currently serves on the University of Houston CIS (Computer Information Systems) Industry Advisory Board, Sam Houston State University Digital and Cyber Forensic Engineering Advisory Board, Lone Star College Cybersecurity and Compute Science Advisory Board, Optiv Customer Advisory Board, InfraGard Houston Chapter Board of Directors, Community Bankers Association Privacy/Data Security Working Group, and several cyber security and technology conference advisory boards.

Previously Marc was a member of the National Infrastructure Protection Plan Working Group and the DHS Threat Information Sharing Framework Working Group and served on the Texas Banker's Association Technology Committee. Marc is a member of InfraGard and previously served as the Deputy Chief for the Houston Chapter Financial Services CSC.

Marc authors articles, presentations and white papers found on LinkedIn and other sources. Marc is the host of a podcast, The CISO Revelation, and is a sought-after speaker, podcast guest, panelist, and moderator at IT and Security conferences.

In 2019, Marc was nominated, selected as a finalist, and won the coveted T.E.N. ISE (Information Security Executive) North America Executive of the Year-Financial Services award.

Also, in 2019, Marc was nominated and selected as a finalist for the T.E.N. ISE Central Executive of the Year award and was nominated for the ISE Central People's Choice award.

In 2018, Marc was nominated and a finalist for the T.E.N. ISE North America Executive of the Year award and the T.E.N. ISE People's Choice award.

In 2016, Marc was nominated and a finalist for the T.E.N. ISE Central Executive of the Year award and T.E.N. ISE Financial Services Executive of the Year award.

CPSIA information can be obtained
at www.ICGtesting.com
Printed in the USA
FSHW010505030321
79135FS